Gretchen Glenny Damo

W9-BHH-784

# LEARNING
# TO CARE

# More Good Year Books® in General Methods and Centers

For information about these or any Good Year Books®, please write to

Good Year Books
Scott, Foresman and Company
1900 East Lake Avenue
Glenview, Illinois 60025

# LEARNING TO CARE
## Classroom Activities for Social and Affective Development

**Norma Deitch Feshbach,**
*University of California, Los Angeles*
**Seymour Feshbach,**
*University of California, Los Angeles*
**Mary Fauvre,**
*California State University, Los Angeles*
**Michael Ballard-Campbell,**
*California State University, Sacramento*

**Scott, Foresman and Company**
Glenview, Illinois  London

ISBN: 0-673-15804-7

Copyright © 1983 Scott, Foresman and Company
All Rights Reserved
Printed in the United States of America

No part of this book may be reproduced in any form or by any means,
except those portions intended for classroom use, without permission in
writing from the publisher.

456 EBI 888786

# PREFACE

Most teachers are concerned about children's social behavior and would like to help them interact effectively with peers and adults. The classroom activities in this book should assist teachers in enhancing children's empathy, social understanding, and social development. As the main educational element of a successful research program at the University of California at Los Angeles (1975–1980) designed to bring about positive changes in children's interpersonal interactions, they were demonstrated to be effective tools in improving children's social behavior.

This volume was written to bridge research findings and the needs of the classroom. The activities are presented for use in both a long-term approach as well as in a more short-term, day-by-day application. In using them, teachers are encouraged to be flexible and make use of their in-depth knowledge of the characteristics of their particular group of children.

We believe that these carefully developed and evaluated activities will result in changes in social behavior that will be valued by teachers, parents, and, ultimately, the children themselves.

# CONTENTS

# INTRODUCTION

## Why the Activities Are Valuable—Practical Reasons

Teachers all seem to agree that more goes on in an "average" day in the classroom than teaching reading, writing, and arithmetic. Something *always* comes up that wasn't covered in the Teacher Education class you took last year, or ten or twenty years ago. It seems that children, parents, and administrators look to the teacher to have all the answers. Whether they like your answers or not, it is important that you have some. Often a classroom dilemma may be about a simple issue such as "Who gets the ball today?" or "They never pick fair teams" or "Johnny said a bad word" or "Someone took my pencil." Teachers usually have standard responses or attitudes for such common and relatively minor problems.

On the other hand, some dilemmas may be more unusual and present problems that are more puzzling and more difficult to resolve. Some days the children seem to be particularly unkind toward one another, or perhaps a minor spat between two children suddenly erupts into a more serious fight. You wonder what became of your efforts to teach responsibility, tolerance, and sensitivity, and wish you had a secret supply of classroom-management techniques and strategies to help you handle their feelings and yours.

Other days are absolutely delightful; everyone seems especially helpful and understanding, a child without a pencil is spontaneously offered one by the other children, or a foot unintentionally placed in the aisle is recognized as just that by the child who tripped. These are the days you treasure—you are pleased at the impact of your message to be understanding of one another, and you go home with your spirits lifted, feeling very proud of your class.

Because children's social skills are erratic and their social sensitivity is often unpredictable, you may long for a method or a ready-made curriculum to help strengthen their interpersonal skills. Such a curriculum could teach children how to develop and build on their social skills by enhancing their understanding of their own feelings and those of others. With a program to follow and some immediate problem-solving techniques to use with the unusual classroom dilemmas, you might have more time to concentrate on reading, arithmetic, and other important subjects. You might even be able to achieve more of the proud, successful feelings at the end of a day and avoid the discouraged, worn-out reaction after a day full of unusual "little" problems and dilemmas.

The activities in this book offer a program that teachers can use in any way that they feel will help them. They were used in both a research project in an educational therapy program and by one of the authors in her fourth-grade classroom to help her deal with day-by-day situations as they arose. She used the activities to deal with student issues and problems such as getting orthodontic braces, being the only new student in the class, being of a different racial background, being teased, and hitting. After one class discussion a girl commented that she felt "some better and some worse"; she knew now that others were misunderstood too, and that made her feel better. But she wished that she hadn't misunderstood and hit another child—that made her feel worse.

The activities are presented both as a whole program to be used throughout the year and as separate adaptations to individual classroom situations when needed. Teachers should find it reassuring to know that they have a set of activities that encourages student social development and helps them cope with some of the more troublesome situations that inevitably occur in all classrooms.

## Why the Activities Are Valuable—Theoretical Reasons

Educators are becoming more interested in the social and emotional behavior of children. One outgrowth of this interest is an increase in the number of curriculum programs devoted to Affective Education, stemming from an awareness of the school's potential role in influencing children's values, perceptions, beliefs, and emotional character. Affective Education concerns an area of children's development that complements but is different from traditional academic education. Children's interests, fears, joys, and anxieties, as well as the problems of growing up and getting along in society, are the subjects of many programs. The curricula are designed to improve children's understanding of their own feelings and behavior and those of others and to enhance rather than replace academic education. It focuses on skills and abilities in social interaction with a goal similar to that of academic education: to help children develop and succeed in today's complex world.

We have come to realize that an understanding of ourselves and others requires the mastery of important cognitive skills. To function effectively in our social world, children must learn that people have intentions, desires, and feelings, even though they cannot be directly observed. As every teacher knows, and as the conflicts that occur daily on the playground demonstrate, children have a great deal of difficulty assuming another person's perspective. The child, to use the term of the great Swiss psychologist Jean Piaget, tends to be *egocentric.* According to Piaget, most six-year-old children find it difficult to view and interpret events separately from their own knowledge and point of view. For example, a typical six-year-old is not likely to understand that being on the playground during recess is not as much fun for a teacher as it is for children. By the time a child is eleven or twelve, he or she is much less egocentric and is better able to understand the viewpoints of others. However, as most teachers know, egocentric behavior does not disappear and may interfere with effective social development well after the child leaves elementary school.

The idea underlying this book is that the child's development of social understanding and social competence can be facilitated by a systematic educational program in much the same manner as the child's development of reading or arithmetic. Thus, the approach to affective education taken in this curriculum places great emphasis on the development of social understanding, or social cognition, as well as on the recognition and mastery of emotional experiences. The development of these affective and cognitive skills should in turn lead to an enhancement of the child's social competence—his or her ability to get along in the world. It should also lead to the development of empathy—the capacity to understand and share the feelings of others. Children who are socially competent and well adjusted learn more easily and readily than children with problems. A successful Affective Education program of the kind presented here can facilitate the acquisition of fundamental academic skills. Ultimately and ideally, such programs can lead to positive, mature behavior and relatively smooth affective growth.

The material in this volume is directed toward children in the early and middle elementary grades. A distinguishing feature of this curriculum is its effort to integrate social understanding with the emotional life of the child. We use the term *empathy* to represent the integration of emotions and social understanding—"the ability to share the affective experience of another person." For example, one child shares another child's sadness

over losing a pet. Empathy and the development of empathic skills depend on three different but related abilities: recognizing emotion, perspective and role taking, and emotional responsiveness. This curriculum is structured around and built on these three abilities. First, an individual must learn to understand what another person is feeling—to recognize and identify another's emotions. Young children often have difficulty interpreting the cues or signs that teachers, as adults, have learned to recognize as happiness, fear, pride, anger, and so forth. Facial expressions, postures, and situational and contextural (background) cues all convey important information that helps an observer understand how someone else is feeling. Although most adults acquire the ability to read such cues in the process of growing up, some children need to be taught this directly. Thus, as a critical component of empathy, identifying feelings should be part of an Affective Education program devoted to the enhancement of social understanding and empathic skills. In this curriculum we have developed activities designed to teach recognition and identification of feelings.

A second component of empathy is the capacity to take the role or perspective of another person. We know from various contradictory reports of fights or scuffles on the playground that children do not always understand both sides of a situation. Therefore we have included activities that help students both experience and understand differing points of view. Assuming the perspective of another person is often cognitively demanding, especially for elementary school children in the earlier grades. For example, to see the world through the eyes of the handicapped child or the new child in the neighborhood requires a cognitive leap from one's own egocentric orientation to the perspective and framework of the other person. Because many children have considerable difficulty in making this cognitive leap, this book gives special attention to sequencing the difficulty of the exercises concerned with perspective and role taking. Role-taking skills, critical to the development of empathy, are also believed to be essential to moral development.

Activities are also drawn from the third component of empathy, emotional responsiveness. These activities give children the opportunity to experience and share feelings. A child's own emotional experience is a major factor in his or her ability to understand and share the emotional experiences of others. These practice exercises do more than help children get in touch with their own feelings; they help children integrate and continue expressing their feelings. The essential components of empathy can be summarized as follows:

1. Recognition and discrimination of feeling — The ability to use relevant information to label and identify emotions

2. Perspective and role taking — The ability to understand that other individuals may see and interpret situations differently; the ability to assume and experience another's viewpoint

3. Emotional responsiveness — The ability to experience and be aware of one's own emotions

## A Note on the Research

The empathy-training curriculum was systematically evaluated as part of an experimental program designed to reduce aggression and antisocial behaviors and foster cooperation and other socially desirable behavior through its implementation. There are many ways of reducing aggression and promoting helpful, cooperative interactions among children. One way is to encourage children to emulate individuals who are socially positive. Another procedure is to rehearse the "do's" and "don'ts" of classroom behavior. A third way is to directly reward children for their positive social behaviors and to discourage or punish negative activities. And a fourth way is to provide children with an understanding of the social world; to help them recognize the differing understandings, desires, and feelings that different people can bring to the same situations.

All four approaches are helpful and necessary. The empathy training curriculum developed at the University of California at Los Angeles is based on the fourth approach. This method was chosen because (1) it deals with both understanding and feelings, (2) it expands the child's awareness of his or her social world, (3) the cognitive and emotional skills it develops can influence many different kinds of social situations, and (4) the type of training it involves can be easily incorporated into a regular classroom curriculum. The evaluation that was carried out supports the statements made about the particular features and advantages of empathy training.

Many steps, some of them time consuming, are involved in the development and evaluation of this curriculum. First, each of the activities was tested with a small group of children. Activities were then revised or discarded, depending on the degree of student interest and the effectiveness of the activity in achieving its objective. After several modifications of each activity, a pilot study was carried out to evaluate the implementation of the entire set of activities over an extended period of time (ten weeks). The children in this pilot study were selected from a predominantly low-income population consisting largely of Anglos and Blacks. Most participants were very aggressive boys and girls, although some nonaggressive children were also included. The children met several times a week in small groups conducted outside the classroom by an instructor working on the project. Measures of aggression and positive social behaviors and of social-understanding and role taking were administered before and after the ten-week period of training, both to the children in the empathy-training groups and to children in control situations. Continuous observations were also made during the course of the ten-week training period.

The results were encouraging. Children in the empathy-training groups had moved in a positive direction and were less aggressive than children in the control groups. Then a more ambitious evaluation with a larger and more representative sample of children was implemented. Finally, on the basis of the additional experience obtained during the pilot study, the exercises were once more revised before the basic evaluation study was conducted.

The main empathy-training program was also carried out over a ten-week period. Groups of six third- and fourth-grade children met with a trainer for a one-hour session three times a week. The children included very aggressive, moderately aggressive, and nonaggressive boys and girls from low- and middle-income groups. Among the ethnic groups represented were Anglos, Blacks, Spanish-speaking Americans, and Orientals. A variety of different measures of *affect, cognition, self-appraisal,* and *social behavior* were again administered before and after the training period. The measures of social behavior included ratings of aggressive and prosocial behaviors by teachers, peers, and the children themselves. The rating scales for aggression included behaviors such as hitting, fighting, saying derogatory remarks, expressing anger, acting in destructive ways, and resisting authority. The prosocial rating scales considered behaviors such as helping, being generous, being sympathetic and sharing. The measures of social understanding and role taking tapped the child's sensitivity to the feelings, perspective, and motivation of characters depicted in experimentally created stories and films. In addition, the children's behavior was continuously observed while they were participating in the exercises. Several times a week during the course of the study the teachers completed behavior checklists for each child.

The children were randomly assigned to empathy-training groups, to problem-solving control activity groups, or to control groups that received the evaluation measures but did not participate in any training activities during the ten-week experimental training period. The problem-solving groups participated in small-group exercises similar to those used for empathy training, but the control activities were oriented toward academic problem solving rather than toward social understanding. The academic problem-solving control training activities were educationally useful, but we did not expect them to have as great an impact on social behavior as the empathy exercises. The problem-solving control group was included to help determine whether any changes produced by empathy training owed to the training exercises or simply to the opportunity to meet and interact in small groups under the supervision of a trained instructor.

Following completion of the training period and data gathering, the findings for the empathy-training groups were then compared with those obtained in the two control groups. The results of these comparisons were generally consistent with the objectives of the empathy-training program. Children in the empathy-training groups developed a better self-concept and displayed greater social understanding than children in either the problem-solving control group or the nonparticipating control group. The children in the empathy-training groups also showed less aggression but so did the children in the problem-solving groups. A more impressive and convincing finding is the difference between the empathy-training and problem-solving control groups in demonstrating positive, or prosocial, behaviors. Figure 1 illustrates the frequency of prosocial behaviors observed by the classroom teachers for the children in each of the three groups. The weeks observed were divided into five periods. Both the problem-solving control group and the nonparticipating control group experienced a *decline* in prosocial behaviors over the experimental period. In contrast, the frequency of prosocial behaviors for the empathy-training groups showed an upward trend and tended to increase during the course of empathy training. The difference between the empathy-training group and each of the control groups is statistically significant. It indicates that empathy training influences the child's social understanding and has a significant influence on the child's social behavior. In addition, empathy training is useful for the average child as well as for the very aggressive child.

For the final phase of the evaluation, the empathy-training activities were instituted in a regular classroom setting. Many of the activities were used with the entire class; others were more appropriate when the class was divided into smaller groups. The children found the activities interesting, and the instructor found them to be very useful.

One should not expect the empathy-training curriculum to work miracles, but the evaluation that was carried out indicates that empathy-training exercises can be a productive and valuable component of elementary school curricula.

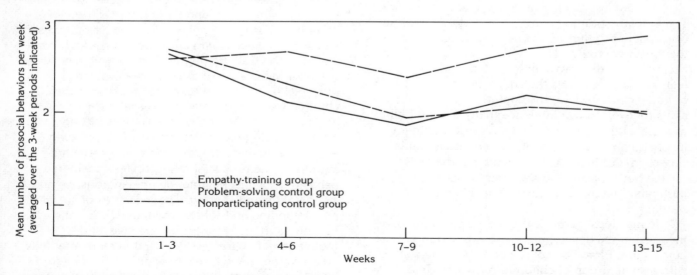

**Figure 1**  Frequency of prosocial behaviors in empathy-training, problem-solving, and non-participating groups.

# HOW TO USE THIS BOOK

The first approach presents the activities for use in a systematic year-long program similar to the training sequences used in the UCLA research project to enhance children's empathy and prosocial behavior. The second approach indicates activities that may be helpful in dealing with situations that can arise at any time.

An important feature of the activities is their flexibility. As the decisionmaker in your classroom you are free to use any or all of them. Some teachers may choose to employ the activities as a supplement to the regular state- or district-adopted social studies program. Other teachers may choose to use the exercises in conjunction with a special unit, such as a unit on feeling or emotions.

We suggest that you begin by reading through all of the activities to get an idea of their range. Some may be more suitable than others for your particular class or group of children. Once you are familiar with all the activities you will be able to set up a program that can be incorporated into your classroom organization. Some of the activities will soon become favorites with the children and can be used on special occasions when you need meaningful activities for short periods of time. An important point to remember is that the activities were developed for classroom use. As the classroom decisionmaker you should feel free to modify the sequence of activities as well as the content of a particular exercise.

## Approach A—A Year-Long Program

### How Are the Activities Sequenced?

The systematic sequence of activities for a year-long program was arranged with several considerations in mind. First, we wanted to balance the content of the activities so that various skills would be introduced early in the curriculum and then repeated later. Second, we balanced the activities by type so that all of the role-playing or art experiences would not come at the same time. Finally, we tried to sequence the activities so that the easiest ones were placed at the beginning. For instance, the children act out less-complicated vignettes (like being a robot) before acting out those demanding greater skills and sophistication.

### With Whom Can the Exercises Be Used?

The activities have been developed and sequenced for children ages seven to eleven. They were initially used with children who were identified by their teacher as having control problems. Since then, they have been used in a regular classroom as well as with children having control problems. One of the important decisions that you will need to make before starting any activities is whether to work with your entire class or with smaller groups. The activities were originally tried with small groups of children who were taken out of their homeroom three times a week for fifty minutes. However, many of the activities have been succesfully carried out with an entire class. The flexibility of the activities should allow you to work with your entire class, smaller groups, or even with individual children. The size of the group will probably influence your choice of activity.

Before starting the activities, you should know the state and local policies regarding the teaching of affective and humanistic curricula that are in effect where you teach. We recommend that you talk to your principal or supervisor and inform him or her of your intentions and objectives. He or she can then guide you about providing information and feedback to parents. Most parents of children with whom we have worked have expressed strong interest in these activities when they were informed of the objectives and of the nature of the curriculum. Inviting parents to observe the training exercises usually elicited an enthusiastic response.

### How Are the Activities Presented?

The activities are presented in the following five-step order.

**1. OBJECTIVES:** We have stated the objectives in terms of behaviors the children will engage in or in terms of intended outcomes, such as developing a skill or ability. Our group leaders found it worthwhile to bear the objectives in mind in order to keep discussions and activities goal related. Perusing the objectives is also a good idea for administrators and parents who are interested in exactly what you are trying to accomplish. Finally, the objectives provide a quick way of determining the usefulness of a particular activity for a special unit you may be planning.

**2. RELATING** the activity to the development of empathy and social skills: Originally, this step was used to help us in developing the activities. It helped us keep on track and to evaluate ideas to determine their relevance to the development of social skills in children. It is a good idea for you to review this item for general background information as well as to help in deciding the sequence of activities you will use in your classroom. You will also be able to determine the specific component of the empathy model by reading the information contained in this item.

**3. MATERIALS:** We attempted to develop activities that do not require much money or time to purchase and prepare. Most of them can be implemented with the materials normally available in a school supply room. But there are some activities that require preparation of special materials or gathering of special supplies. Quickly reading this item will enable you to prepare in sufficient time.

**4. PROCEDURE:** This section describes the instructions for each activity in a step-by-step manner. Discussion questions and examples of specific points in the exercise are usually listed, but you should feel free to generate your own as well. This section also outlines the method we found to be most successful for each activity, but we expect that you will naturally adapt it to your own style and to meet your own needs.

**4. SPECIAL HINTS:** Another name for this section might be "Tips for Teachers." It contains all the thoughts and observations that do not fit under other headings. It was added as a result of discussions with our research staff, and it generally indicates additional things to watch for within each activity. For example, if special emphasis on a particular topic during a discussion is important, we have mentioned it under "Special hints." Or if our group leaders had some good ideas for preparing the activity, we listed them here. We have also indicated which activities are appropriate for use more than once, and which exercises require the most control or guidance from the teacher.

## Approach B—Pinch Hitting— As the Need Arises

As noted earlier, every teacher faces situations or behaviors that he or she doesn't know how to handle or react to. A teacher may be unsure of what to do when a child is being picked on or teased by the other children. Most teachers have experienced incidents in which one child says one thing, another says something quite different, and both are certain that the other is lying. Neither is aware that they may have seen the same event in different ways. For many years teachers have asked administrators, specialists, and other educators to provide them with suggestions and activities to handle these types of situations as they arise in the classroom.

The "Activities for Use in Problem Situations" table provides some suggestions for use when teachers are face to face with troublesome situations in the classroom or on the playground. This approach differs from Approach A, in which activities are presented in a more structured, long-term sequence for regular use. The suggestions came from one fourth-grade teacher's experiences with the activities over the course of a school year. She found that one of the best ways to help children understand how others feel and improve their social skills is to spend classroom time on problems as they arise from the children's natural and spontaneous interactions. For example, if a teacher notices that the children are not being sensitive or aware of the feelings of others, he or she could use the activities that develop the ability to recognize the emotions and feelings of others. It makes sense to use the activities at the time the problem or situation arises so that the children will have a better understanding of the event and its meaning for their own lives.

The following situation occurred in the course of normal classroom activity, and it prompted the teacher to put some of the activities listed in this book to work as events occurred. Evidently something had upset one of the boys playing kickball at morning recess, and he angrily lashed out at a boy with glasses, shouting, "Out of my way, foureyes," as he pushed him in the face and popped one lense out of the glasses. The angry boy ran off to the classroom, the hurt boy wilted in frightened tears, and a boy who had seen it all happen ran to the teacher. He tried to tell her what had occurred, but he was crying too. It took some time to establish that his tears showed empathy for the boy with the broken glasses, and that he was not in fact hurt physically. Although he didn't understand the cause of the first boy's anger, he certainly knew how it felt to be teased. The teacher was able to use several of the exercises to provide the children with insights about this event.

The following table is by no means complete, but it can be expanded by a teacher working in his or her own classroom who has a better understanding of the needs of a particular group of children.

| Problem | Examples | Exercises |
|---|---|---|
| Two people see the same event but tell different stories as seen from their own perspectives. | "Joe started it!" <br> "Susie called him a bad word first!" <br> "That is *not* what happened." <br> "I saw it all, and _____." <br> "That's so dumb, _____." <br> "No, the guy was *tall*." | Vase/Face (p. 10) <br> Short and Tall (p. 10) <br> The Biggest Bear (p. 12) <br> Telling Stories from Various Points of View (p. 14) <br> Role Playing from Photographs (p. 14) <br> Late Arriver (p. 22) <br> Pick a Present for Your Partner (p. 26) <br> Guided Walk (p. 19) <br> Rufus (p. 23) <br> Acting Out Opposites (p. 17) <br> Problem Stories (pp. 20, 24, 27) <br> Step-by-Step Perspective Drawing (p. 24) |
| Understanding why people behave in a certain way. | "Look at her! She's so stupid, she would do _____." <br> "Why is he crying?" <br> "What's so funny?" <br> "What did you do *that* for?" <br> "You dummy, that's not for _____." <br> "Why won't she _____?" | The Biggest Bear (p. 12) <br> Role Playing from Photographs (p. 14) <br> How Would You Feel? (p. 15) <br> What Ifs and Mysteries (p. 18) <br> Can You Guess What Makes Me Feel? (p. 20) <br> Levels of Emotional Intensity (p. 22) <br> Late Arriver (p. 22) <br> Rufus (p. 23) <br> Emotions in a Hat (p. 26) |
| Looking carefully at or attending to another person. | "But she didn't *look* sad." <br> "How was I supposed to know you were angry?" <br> "Nobody told me he was upset." | Make a Face and Pass It On (p. 13) <br> Identifying Facial Expressions in Photographs (p. 11) <br> Role Playing from Photographs (p. 14) |
| Improving social communication skills by counteracting reputations. | "But Billy is such a brain, why should he cry?" <br> "She's so clumsy, she couldn't draw that." | Name That Kid (p. 14) |
| Improving listening skills and working together in a group. | "Hey, no way. That's not what I said." <br> "Shut up! *I'm* talking." <br> "He's lying. I didn't say that!" | Telephone (p. 9) <br> Referential Communication Games (pp. 10, 15) <br> Tape Recording with a Partner (p. 24) |
| Giving and following directions. | "But Mrs. _____, you never told us to do _____." <br> "What page? What book?" <br> "I don't get it." <br> "Hey. I thought you meant _____." | Telephone (p. 9) <br> Referential Communication Games (pp. 10, 15) <br> Mirroring (p. 11) |
| Understanding how misunderstandings arise from miscommunication. | "That's *not* what I said." <br> "He's so dumb, he always _____." | Telephone (p. 9) <br> Rufus (p. 23) |
| Recognizing how another person feels. | "Well how was I supposed to know he was sad?" <br> "I can't tell whether or not you're happy." <br> "I didn't know she was *that* mad!" <br> "But I thought you said, 'Go ahead.' How was I supposed to know you didn't mean it?" | Magazine Collage (p. 9) <br> Guess your Friend's Feeling (p. 17) <br> Taking Photos, Making Cards (p. 16) <br> Identifying Facial Expressions in Photographs (p. 11) <br> Felt Faces (p. 12) <br> Concentration (p. 16) <br> Tape Recordings (pp. 18, 23, 24) <br> Taking Group Pictures (p. 20) <br> Levels of Emotional Intensity (p. 22) |

The following table groups activities according to the type of empathy-related ability they help develop: recognition and discrimination of emotion, perspective and role taking, and emotional responsiveness. These groupings show that many of the activities are addressed to more than one ability, and they should allow greater flexibility in selecting and sequencing activities for use in your own classroom.

### Activities Grouped by Type of Empathy-Related Ability

| Ability | Activities |
|---|---|
| Recognition and discrimination of emotion | 1, 2, 7, 8 10, 13, 14, 18, 19, 20, 25, 31, 33, 35, 37 |
| Perspective and role taking | 3, 4, 5, 6 9, 11, 12, 15, 16, 17, 21, 22, 23, 24, 26, 27, 28, 29, 30, 32, 34, 36, 38, 39, 41, 42, 43, 44 |
| Emotional responsiveness | 10, 18, 22, 23 25, 30, 31, 33, 35, 40, 43 |

# Resources

**Castillo, G.** *Left-Handed Teaching.* New York: Holt, Rinehart and Winston, 1978.

**Chandler, M.** "Egocentrism and Antisocial Behavior: The Assessment and Training of Social Perspective Taking Skills." *Developmental Psychology* 9 (1973): 326–332.

**Encyclopaedia Britannica Films.** *Late for Dinner—Was Dawn Right?*

**Feshbach, N.** "Studies of Empathic Behavior in Children." In *Progress in Experimental Personality Research,* vol. 8, edited by B. A. Maher. New York: Academic Press, 1978, pp. 1–47.

**Feshbach, N.** "Empathy Training: A Field Study in Affective Education." In *Aggression and Behavior Change: Biological and Social Processes,* edited by S. Feshbach and A. Fraczek. New York: Praeger, 1979, pp. 234–249.

**Feshbach, N. D.,** and **S. Feshbach.** "Empathy Training and the Regulation of Aggression: Potentialities and Limitations." *Academic Psychological Bulletin* 4, no. 3 (1982): 399–413.

**Instructo Reference Materials for Identifying Facial Expressions, no. 1215.** *Understanding Our Feelings.* Paoli, Pa.: Instructo Corporation.

**Palomares, V.** *A Curriculum on Conflict Management.* Palo Alto, Calif.: Human Development Training Institute, 1975.

**Schweitzer, B. B.** *Amigo.* New York: Macmillan, 1963.

**Shaftel, R.,** and **G. Shaftel.** *Role Playing for Social Values, Decision Making in the Social Studies.* Englewood Cliffs, N.J.: Prentice-Hall, 1967.

**Shaftel, F.,** and **G. Shaftel.** *People in Action,* Role-Playing and Discussion Photographs for Elementary Social Studies, Level D. New York: Holt, Rinehart and Winston, 1970.

**Ward, L.** *The Biggest Bear.* New York: Scholastic Book Services, 1975.

# ACTIVITIES

## 1
## Telephone

**1. OBJECTIVES:** To improve listening abilities and to help children see some causes of poor communication. Specifically, to participate in a game in which children listen to and repeat a sentence.

**2. RELATIONSHIP** to the development of empathy: The ability to communicate well is necessary for effective interaction in any group. In addition, discriminating affect requires the children to observe each other closely.

**3. MATERIALS:** Chalk and chalkboard.

**4. PROCEDURE:** Have the children sit in a straight line, side by side. Start by whispering a simple sentence to the first child in line. Each child in turn whispers the sentence to the next child in line. The last child repeats the sentence out loud. Write this version on the board. Next write the original sentence on the board, and have the children discuss whether there are any differences in the two sentences. Next, start the process over by having a child make up the sentence. Each child should tell you what his or her sentence is. Challenge the children to make as few errors in communication as possible.

**5. SPECIAL HINTS:** Remember to start off with a simple sentence. Encourage discussion of where and how the communication errors came about. This game may take only five to ten minutes, but the discussion of causes of miscommunication may be referred to in explaining future disagreements between children. It can be played at different times throughout the year.

## 2
## Magazine Collage

**1. OBJECTIVES:** To reinforce concepts and cues related to emotions. Specifically, create a group magazine collage composed of pictures related to a particular emotion.

**2. RELATIONSHIP** to the development of empathy: Labeling and discriminating affect by reading social and facial cues from pictures.

**3. MATERIALS:** Magazines with many pictures of people; scissors; glue; two pieces of butcher paper.

**4. PROCEDURE:** Explain to the children that they will form two groups and work on a collage composed of pictures that convey an emotion they have chosen (happy, sad, angry, and so forth). After the two groups are chosen, they are to move to separate parts of the room and work on their collages. Children should try to cover most of the butcher paper with pictures related to the theme emotion. Hopefully, the two groups will choose different theme emotions. When the collages are finished, children meet together as a single group to share their collages. Without identifying their chosen emotion, each subgroup tries to guess the theme emotion of the other subgroup. The discussion should center on what aspects of the pictures helped the children to determine the theme emotion of the other group. Collages should be kept and displayed in the room.

**5. SPECIAL HINTS:** Keep the two groups working separately as they complete the collages, and encourage discussion emphasizing the use of the social and facial cues provided in the pictures. This could be used as a continuing project at a center or workshop area, for developing a whole-class collage, or for making individual collages.

# Referential Communication— Game I

**1. OBJECTIVES:** To learn that communicating information requires clear explanations and careful listening. Specifically, to take turns giving directions and asking questions in order to complete a ditto.

**2. RELATIONSHIP** to the development of empathy: Assuming the perspective of another by understanding the need for supplying missing information in communicating directions.

**3. MATERIALS:** Crayons, two blank design dittos. (See pp. 31–32.)

**4. PROCEDURE:** Have the children sit in a large circle facing out, with writing boards on the floor or in their laps. Ask one child at a time to direct the group regarding which part of the design is to be colored. The first child describes the first element to be colored, for example, "Color the triangle on the left side green." The next child describes the next element, and so forth, until the design is complete. Listeners must ask specific questions to clarify directions. Children must not look at each other's pictures until the end of the activity, so there must be enough room between children. When the activity is over, have the children compare their pictures to see how well they followed directions. You might ask: Was it easier to give directions or to follow directions? What was hard about it?

**5. SPECIAL HINTS:** Before starting the activity, encourage the group to talk about the design, and help them label shapes and specific spaces as necessary. You might give an example or two for the group, with everyone finding the correct space together. It is important to encourage the children to ask questions if they do not understand one another's directions.

# Vase/Face, Duck/Rabbit, Old Woman/Young Woman

**1. OBJECTIVES:** To perceive and discuss differing visual perspectives. Specifically, to view three drawings in which two hidden objects may be found.

**2. RELATIONSHIP** to the development of empathy: Assuming the perspective of another person.

**3. MATERIALS:** Two copies each of the vase/face and duck/rabbit drawings; an old woman/young woman drawing for each child. (See pp. 33–35.)

**4. PROCEDURE:** Divide the group in half. Starting with the vase/face drawing, tell one group that they will see a picture of a white vase. Then show them a copy of the picture with the vase outlined in ink, concealing it from the other group. Tell the other group that they are going to see a picture of the profiles of two black faces, and then show them the picture with the black faces outlined in ink. (Pretend that you are showing a different picture to each group). Next, show the entire group the vase/face drawing and ask the children to tell what they see. Discuss why they see different pictures, and ask them to show each other what they see. Repeat the process with the duck/rabbit picture. Pass out copies of the old woman/young woman drawing. Ask the children to find the two pictures without identifying them in advance.

**5. SPECIAL HINTS:** Make sure to pretend that you are showing different pictures. Encourage the children to change perspectives in order to see both drawings. If they can't, ask the other children to help.

# Short and Tall

**1. OBJECTIVES:** To learn that height affects the ability to do different tasks or to see different things. Specifically, to assume various heights and walk through a specially prepared display.

**2. RELATIONSHIP** to the development of empathy: Preliminary skill to perspective taking.

**3. MATERIALS:** Height chart (a chart showing pictures of tall and short individuals and showing how height affects occupation, for example, pictures of Wilt Chamberlain and pictures of jockeys, tree trimmers and so forth); height blocks; objects such as a mirror, pictures, a water pitcher, cups, a shelf, paper, and scissors, placed at various heights.

**4. PROCEDURE:** Begin by discussing differences in height. Have the children divide themselves into "tall" and "short" groups, and then have them line up in order. Ask one child to check their order. Discuss relative "tallness" and "shortness" of adults or children much younger than they are.

Set up a part of the room with five or six "stations" where the children can perform certain tasks or observe various objects. For example, place the mirrors too high for them, place a plant too high to be watered easily, hang a picture too low, put the water pitcher and cups too high, or put paper and scissors on a very low table.

Have the children take turns going through the "stations," once wearing the height blocks and once "walking" on their knees. They should remember which tasks were easy or hard when they were "tall" or "short." As time and interest permit, they might do the tasks at their normal height as well.

When all have done the tasks at different heights, assemble the group to discuss which tasks were made easier or more difficult as a result of being various heights.

Finally, discuss tasks or competencies in general as they relate to height. The height chart provides examples, but children should be encouraged to suggest examples from their own experiences. You might ask: How did Wilt the Stilt's height affect his career choice? How did Tom Thumb get his name? Why are chairs in a nursery school small?

**5. SPECIAL HINT:** Emphasize the concept of "point of view." In this activity, various physical and literal points of view result from being different heights. Later activities focus on more abstract points of view in which opinions differ based on differing informational or philosophical perspectives.

# Mirroring*

**1. OBJECTIVES:** To improve observation skills. Specifically, to participate in a game in which a partner's behavior is imitated.

**2. RELATIONSHIP** to the development of empathy: Preliminary skill to perspective.

**3. MATERIALS:** None.

**4. PROCEDURE:** Have the children sit in two rows, facing each other. One row plays "Actors," the other row plays "Mirrors." "Mirrors" must imitate "Actors'" behavior exactly, copying every action. Rows then switch roles—"Mirrors" become "Actors," initiating the behavior. Encourage children to start with simple, short actions and progress to more difficult and complex behaviors.

**5. SPECIAL HINT:** This activity may be done on several occasions, or it may be repeated on the same day. It should not take more than ten to fifteen minutes for one session.

# Identifying Facial Expressions in Photographs

**1. OBJECTIVES:** To read facial cues and to suggest various interpretations for causes of affect. Specifically, to identify and discuss emotional aspects of situations presented in photographs.

**2. RELATIONSHIP** to the development of empathy: Discriminating and labeling affect.

**3. MATERIALS:** Set of Instructo photographs, "Understanding Our Feelings," or other appropriate photos.

**4. PROCEDURE:** Begin by asking children to name some feelings, and write this list on the board. Have the children identify the emotional states of the characters in the photographs. If opinions differ, discuss why. For each photograph, the children should offer several alternatives as to

*From *Left-Handed Teaching: Lessons in Affective Education,* 2nd ed. by Gloria A. Castillo. Copyright © 1974 by Praeger Publishers, Copyright © 1978 by Holt, Rinehart and Winston. Reprinted by permission of Holt, Rinehart and Winston, CBS College Publishing.

what might have caused the character to feel the emotion pictured.

As the emotions in the photographs are labeled, you might group the photos showing the same emotion and then compare the degree of emotion within each group. You might ask: How does this person feel? What might have made him or her feel this way? What other reasons can you think of?

**5. SPECIAL HINTS:** Encourage the children to suggest alternatives to or causes for a particular emotional state. They might describe events that happened to them that are similar to those suggested for the causes of the feelings described in the pictures.

# Butcher-Paper Puzzle

**1. OBJECTIVES:** To promote group cohesiveness and interaction. Specifically, to participate in an art project in which individual drawings are organized around a central theme (emotion).

**2. RELATIONSHIP** to the development of empathy: Group cohesiveness is necessary to successfully complete future exercises; expressing and labeling affect.

**3. MATERIALS:** Large (3 ft. by 5 ft.) piece of butcher paper or newsprint; crayons.

**4. PROCEDURE:** Cut the piece of paper into smaller, odd-shaped pieces, giving one to each child. Decide with the group what emotion will be the theme. Then have each child decorate his or her piece of paper to complement the theme emotion. The children may choose to draw a whole scene or an object, or they may merely color the page. When the pictures are complete, reconstruct the large piece by taping the smaller pieces of paper together. The finished product is a result of all the children's work combined. It can be used as room decoration.

**5. SPECIAL HINT:** This activity can be treated like the Magazine Collage activity, with two groups working separately. Each group must reconstruct the other's puzzle and guess the other's theme. This can also be done as a whole-class project, using a large sheet of butcher paper. (The puzzles are easier to reconstruct if a key is made when the pieces are cut apart).

# The Biggest Bear

**1. OBJECTIVES:** To increase understanding of the motives, intentions, and perspectives of other people. Specifically, to listen to a story and consider alternative viewpoints and solutions.

**2. RELATIONSHIP** to the development of empathy: Assuming the perspectives of characters in the story.

**3. MATERIALS:** Ward, L. *The Biggest Bear.* (New York: Scholastic Book Services, 1975).

**4. PROCEDURE:** Introduce this activity by asking the children to keep the following questions in mind as the story is being read:

How do the various characters feel about the bear? Why?

Why do the neighbors hate the bear?

What else could have been done to solve the problem in the story?

How did you feel during the story?

If you were the child in the story what would you have done?

If you were the child in the story how would you have felt?

Has anything like this ever happened to you?

Read the story to the children. After the story is read, discussion should focus on providing answers to the above questions.

**5. SPECIAL HINTS:** Be sure to prepare the children for the story by asking the questions mentioned above. It is important to stress the differing perspectives of the characters in the story. Other stories involving differing perspectives can be used in a similar fashion, discussing the feelings and points of view of the various characters.

# Felt Faces

**1. OBJECTIVES:** To learn the relationship between facial expressions and feelings. Specifically, to construct faces out of felt pieces to portray various feelings.

**2. RELATIONSHIP** to the development of empathy: Labeling and discriminating affect by reading social (facial) cues in a stylized, specific context; encouraging emotional responsiveness.

**3. MATERIALS:** Individual felt boards (one for you and one for each child) with several parts of a face cut out, to be added to an oval shape to make a face (like Mr. Potato Man). Pieces may be stylized or realistic, but there should be several choices for each part of the face (eyes, noses, eyebrows, and mouths) so as to convey a range of feelings—happiness, anger, sadness, surprise, and so forth.

**4. PROCEDURE:** Have the children sit in a circle, facing out, so that they cannot see each other's felt boards. They then construct a face as you or a child calls out a theme feeling, for example, "Make a sad face." After each feeling sentence has been stated, have the children show their "pictures." You might ask: What parts of the picture show the feeling (mouth, eyes, eyebrows)? Do different parts of the face show different feelings?

*Variations:* You might show one happy or angry face and ask the children to show the same emotion in a different way. The children might make their own faces and let others guess what feeling their face shows.

**5. SPECIAL HINTS:** Encourage the children to take turns providing feeling words for making faces. It might help to list the emotions on the board.

# Charades

**1. OBJECTIVES:** To develop the prerequisite skills necessary for more advanced role playing. Specifically, to act out noncomplex, nonpersonal situations.

**2. RELATIONSHIP** to the development of empathy: Assuming the role of another.

**3. MATERIALS:** Cards on which various simple situations or objects (a robot or a bicycle rider, for example) are depicted.

**4. PROCEDURE:** Place the cards in an envelope. Ask the children to sit in a circle. Have each child choose one card from the envelope, concealing it from the other children. The child then acts out the situation or objects depicted on the card. Whoever correctly guesses the situation or objects gets the next turn. The game continues until the children want to stop or become bored, or until all of the cards have been used.

**5. SPECIAL HINTS:** The children can use any clues, as long as they do not explicitly mention the name of the situation or object. For instance, if a cat is on one of the cards, it is okay to meow or to pretend to be scratching with claws. Attempt to give the children an even number of turns as actors. The children might think of their own situations after the cards have been used up. This activity can be repeated on different occasions, depending on the level of interest expressed by the group.

# Silhouettes

**1. OBJECTIVES:** To promote cooperation and interaction. Specifically, to produce silhouettes to be used in decorating the room.

**2. RELATIONSHIP** to the development of empathy: Developing group cooperation; taking another person's perspective.

**3. MATERIALS:** Filmstrip projector, black construction paper, white construction paper, masking tape, scissors, pencils.

**4. PROCEDURE:** Have the students choose partners. Focus the light from the projector on a piece of black construction paper taped on the chalkboard. Have one student sit in front of the black paper, displaying his or her profile. Then his or her partner traces the shadow cast on the paper. After both partners have had their profiles drawn, they should cut them out and mount the silhouettes on white paper.

**5. SPECIAL HINTS:** Encourage the children to take their time when tracing the profiles. You may need to help in the tracing process.

# Make a Face and Pass It On

**1. OBJECTIVES:** To improve observation and communication skills. Specifically, to play a game in which children focus on and imitate another child's facial expression.

**2. RELATIONSHIP** to the development of empathy: Discriminating and labeling affective states in others.

**3. MATERIALS:** None.

**4. PROCEDURE:** Have the children sit in a straight line, all facing the same way. Tell them that they're going to play the game of "Telephone," but without talking. The person who starts the game thinks of a feeling and then makes a face to show that feeling. He or she then passes that face on to the next person, who looks at the face carefully and then passes it on as well. The last person guesses the feeling of the person who began the game. Then the person who started the game gets to tell whether the others are right. You should provide a practice emotion by saying, "Let's practice by having the first person make a happy face. Remember to look carefully at the face made by the person before you and pass on the same face to the child after you." After each round, have the children change places in the line so that everyone has the opportunity to both initiate and pass on expressions.

**5. SPECIAL HINTS:** Practice a few expressions before the children start on their own. Encourage the children to discuss why the last child may have incorrectly identified the emotion portrayed by the first child. This game works better when children are seated.

# Name That Kid*

**1. OBJECTIVES:** To increase listening and observation skills. Specifically, to create and listen to clues to identify the secret person.

**2. RELATIONSHIP** to the development of empathy: Discriminating and labeling affect.

**3. MATERIALS:** Instructo photos or other appropriate photos.

**4. PROCEDURE:** Introduce this activity as a guessing game in which one member of the group provides a clue that will enable the other children to identify a specific child. For example, "I'm thinking of a child who has freckles." As the children gain understanding of the game, the clues should become more sophisticated. "I'm thinking of a child who has freckles and doesn't like to play baseball," for example. The child who identifies the secret person then gives the next clue. After the children are familiar with the procedure, introduce the second part of the activity. Display Instructo photos on a chalk tray (or in some appropriate place) and continue guessing, including the photos to expand the number of choices available. The person giving the clues may describe a photo *or* a member of the group. Encourage the children to imitate the emotions shown in the photos in order to make the game more complex. Alternate photos on the chalk tray.

**5. SPECIAL HINTS:** Children may use negatives to describe each other—fat, dumb, and so forth—so keep close track of the discussion, and emphasize that descriptions should be positive.

# Role Playing from Photographs*

**1. OBJECTIVES:** To enhance role-playing skills. Specifically, to act out various roles depicted in photographs.

**2. RELATIONSHIP** to the development of empathy: Assuming the role of another.

**3. MATERIALS:** Photographs that depict dilemmas, conflicts, or problems. Good photographs to use are selections 2, 3, 5, and 6 from *People in Action.*

**4. PROCEDURE:** Have the children role play each scene several times, acting out the proposed solutions that seem to evoke the most interest and enthusiasm. Discuss consequences of the various solutions offered. Emphasize generating many alternatives, not on selecting one "best" solution.

**5. SPECIAL HINTS:** Be sure to review the pages in the teacher's guide before leading this activity.

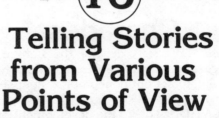

# Telling Stories from Various Points of View

**1. OBJECTIVES:** To develop understanding of different points of view. Specifically, to listen to and discuss stories in which different points of view are emphasized.

**2. RELATIONSHIP** to the development of empathy: Assuming the perspective of another.

**3. MATERIALS:** "Joey" stories (see p. 36) and *Amigo,* by B. B. Schweitzer (New York: Macmillan, 1963).

**4. PROCEDURE:** Discuss the concept of point of view. Elicit examples from the children about watching a fight or about a teacher's opinion of what happened in class versus a child's opinion. Read the three versions of "Joey," and ask what is

---

*Adapted from G. Castillo, *Left-Handed Teaching* (New York: Holt, Rinehart and Winston, 1978.

*Adapted from F. Shaftel and G. Shaftel, *People in Action,* Role-Playing and Discussion Photographs for Elementary Social Studies, Level D (New York: Holt, Rinehart and Winston), 1970.

different about each story. Ask the children to try to figure out from whose point of view each story is told: *who* is each story about? (The *whats* and *whens* of each story are the same.) The children should begin to understand the concept of point of view—seeing an event through another person's eyes. Read *Amigo,* and ask whose point of view is taken in the story (the boy wants a dog, and the dog wants a boy). Have the children indicate changes in point of view as the story progresses.

**5. SPECIAL HINTS:** Point of view is generally a difficult concept for children. It is best to get lots of examples from them at the beginning, if possible.

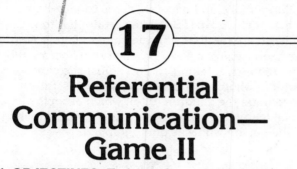

# 17

# Referential Communication— Game II

**1. OBJECTIVES:** To learn that communicating information requires clear explanations and careful questions. Specifically, to take turns giving directions and asking questions in order to complete a ditto.

**2. RELATIONSHIP** to the development of empathy: Assuming the perspective of another by understanding the need for supplying missing information in communicating directions.

**3. MATERIALS:** Crayons or blocks, blank design pages. (See pp. 37–38.)

**4. PROCEDURE:** Have the children sit in a large circle facing out, with writing boards on the floor or in their laps. Ask one child at a time to direct the group regarding which part of the design is to be colored (or covered with blocks). The listeners must ask specific questions to clarify the directions. The children should not look at each other's pictures until the end of the activity, so they should sit far enough apart. When the activity is over, have the children compare their pictures to see how successful they were. You might ask: Was it easier to give directions or to follow directions? What was hard about it?

**5. SPECIAL HINTS:** Before starting this activity, encourage the group to talk about the design, helping them label shapes and specific spaces as necessary. You might give an example or two for the group, with everyone finding the correct space together. It is important to encourage the children to ask questions if they do not understand the directions given by another child.

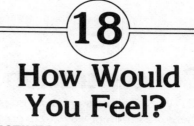

# 18

# How Would You Feel?

**1. OBJECTIVES:** To interpret an emotional situation. Specifically, to identify one's own emotional response as well as to anticipate another's.

**2. RELATIONSHIP** to the development of empathy: Discriminating and labeling affect in others, facilitated by awareness and expression of feeling in oneself, in order to enhance emotional responsiveness.

**3. MATERIALS:** List of events.

**4. PROCEDURE:** Read the first five statements and ask each child how he or she would feel if the situation happened to him or her.

Then read the last nine events, asking the whole group to decide how they think a classmate would feel. (Let each child have a chance to be the "target child.") Be sure to emphasize the *other person's* feelings. Ask for different opinions, and then ask the target child to verify.

**5. SPECIAL HINTS:** If all the children give the same response, ask them to think of reasons why another response might be appropriate. For example, if all the children answer "sad" in response to "Your friend broke his leg," suggest "happy"—the friend would not have to mow the lawn.

### *List of Events*

1. Your friend broke his leg.
2. You are elected class president.
3. You won first place in a race.
4. Your brother is sick and can't go with you to the beach.
5. School is canceled for the day.
6. You are late for class.
7. Your mother gets a new car.
8. You have a big part in the class play.
9. You are alone in the house.
10. You lost your homework.
11. You find a dollar.
12. You are invited to a party.
13. You are not chosen for the school team.
14. You are invited to a baseball game.

# 19
# Concentration

**1. OBJECTIVES:** To focus on facial cues and to learn that there are different ways to express emotions. Specifically, to match emotions that are portrayed on game-card pictures.

**2. RELATIONSHIP** to the development of empathy: Discriminating and labeling affect.

**3. MATERIALS:** Deck of cards with either pictures or emotion words on one side. Duplicates of pictures can be matched, or children can match pictures with words.

**4. PROCEDURE:** Place cards with the pictures or words face down. Each child turns two cards over. If the cards match (show the same emotion), the child removes the cards from the game. The cards that do not match are turned face down and left on the board. The person who gets the most matches (and cards) wins the game.

**5. SPECIAL HINTS:** "Cards" can be made from magazine pictures that have been pasted onto small index cards. Children might be able to help in cutting out pictures and collecting faces showing strong emotion.

# 20
# Taking Photos, Making Cards

**1. OBJECTIVES:** To photograph the children portraying various emotions; to verbalize ideas about which facial features communicate affective information. Specifically, to photograph children while they are portraying various emotions.

**2. RELATIONSHIP** to the development of empathy: Discriminating and labeling affective cues.

**3. MATERIALS:** Polaroid camera and film; construction paper, scissors, glue, felt markers, decorative stickers.

**4. PROCEDURE:** Tell the children that they are going to be actors. Ask them to think up several names for emotions that they will portray for the camera. Ask, "What are some feelings that people show on their faces?" List the suggestions on the board. The children then choose one of the emotions and practice portraying it a few times. Take a picture of each child as he or she stands on

a line previously marked on the ground. The children should portray their emotion for the camera. Next, show the children how the pictures are developed, counting to sixty for each photograph. Tell the children not to touch the photos. Place all of the photos on a table top, and ask the children to look at the expressions on their faces. See whether the children are able to match each photo with a feeling word listed on the board.

Ask the children to act out examples of how to exaggerate the feelings portrayed in the photos, for example, happier, sadder, and so forth. After a brief discussion, and when the photos are dry, have the children make and decorate cards to take home.

**5. SPECIAL HINTS:** Make certain that the children are familiar with the camera before starting the exercise. Take a few practice shots before the children arrive, taking care to adjust the exposure. Outdoor photos are usually most successful. Encourage the children to tell which aspects of facial features communicate the emotional feeling of the person who was photographed.

# 21
# Camera Walk

**1. OBJECTIVES:** To understand that space looks different from different locations. Specifically, to draw a picture of an object indicated nonverbally by another child.

**2. RELATIONSHIP** to the development of empathy: Assuming the perspective of another; observing and interpreting the expectations and choices of another.

**3. MATERIALS:** "Camera" bag or box with "lense hole" for children to wear, paper and various materials for drawing, various articles displayed for "photographing."

**4. PROCEDURE:** Have the group sit in a circle, eyes closed, listening to the sounds in the room. After a minute or so, have the children discuss the sounds they heard. Again have the children close their eyes, and ask them to picture in their minds what they would see if they were looking directly ahead. Emphasize attending to details. You may ask the children to look again and then tell from memory what is around them. Next, have the children go on a "camera walk." The children should work together in pairs without talking. One child puts on the "camera" bag or box and pretends to be the "camera." The other child is the photographer. The photographer leads the "camera" around the room and squeezes the "camera's" hand when the photographer wants to take a picture. Encourage the children to take "photos" of the arrangements set up around the room for this purpose. After a picture has been taken, have the pairs come back to the circle, and have each child draw a picture of the scene "photographed," or of one that should have been "photographed." The children should then have a chance to compare their pictures and to discuss their memories of what the picture should have looked like—of what should have been "photographed." The children should go on a second camera walk, trading roles, and repeating the process.

**5. SPECIAL HINTS:** Suggest that the children avoid looking at their partner's drawing until the drawings are both finished. Suggest to the "camera" that he or she look carefully at what the photographer is looking at when the "camera" is "clicked." The perspective and angle of the drawings should be as accurate as possible, but artistic skill should not be compared.

# Acting Out Opposites

**1. OBJECTIVES:** To improve role-playing skills. Specifically, to act out different situations from opposite perspectives.

**2. RELATIONSHIP** to the development of empathy: Assuming the role of another; encouraging emotional responsiveness.

**3. MATERIALS:** Deck of situation cards in a bag. (See "Special hints.")

**4. PROCEDURE:** Inform the children that they are going to be actors. Say, "In this bag are lots of different cards that describe situations for you to act out. After you choose a card, read only one side—the side that is up when you pull the card out of the bag. Then act out what the card says. Keep acting until I tell you to stop; then give your card to another person in the group. That person will turn the card over and act out what is written on the other side." Offer the bag to the first child, who should act out the written situation and pass the card on to the next child. The audience guesses after both situations on a card have been acted. After each card, discuss the following points:

a. What the card said. (Have the actors confirm any guesses.)
b. How they guessed what was being acted out.
c. How the child demonstrated the situation.
d. Whether anyone knows what the word *opposite* means. (This should be a brief discussion.)

**5. SPECIAL HINTS:** The children may need help thinking of ways to act out the situations. Your role should be supportive and helpful in terms of suggestions for action.

The cards might say:

a. Going somewhere you love to go
   Going somewhere you hate to go
b. Coming home from a fun day
   Coming home from a rotten day
c. Listening to someone praise you
   Listening to someone criticize you
d. Eating something you like
   Eating something you hate
e. Reading a book that is funny
   Reading a book that is stupid
f. Watching a television show that is interesting
   Watching a television show that is boring
g. Smelling something delicious
   Smelling something awful
h. Touching something that feels nice and soft
   Touching something that feels slimy
i. Listening to beautiful music
   Listening to horrible, screechy noise
j. Being told good news
   Being told bad news

# Guess Your Friend's Feeling

**1. OBJECTIVES:** To focus on nonfacial body cues that communicate a particular feeling. Specifically, to act out and identify various feelings.

**2. RELATIONSHIP** to the development of empathy: By placing the children in an observer role, they will practice discriminating affective states in others; encouraging emotional responsiveness.

**3. MATERIALS:** Deck of cards with the names of emotions written on the cards, stop watch, paper sack.

**4. PROCEDURE:** Two teams of players are to act out emotions nonverbally, sitting across a table or a circle from one another. One player draws a card with the name of an emotion written on it. Next, the player covers his or her face with a bag, or holds a paper in front of his or her face. Then, without speaking, the player should act out the emotion written on the card. The child from the opposing team who guesses the correct answer may act out the next card. The teams have a total of thirty seconds to correctly identify the emotion. Players must start with the paper sack on, and two points are earned if the opponent can guess the feeling from body cues. If the paper sack is removed, only one point is earned. But thirty seconds is the limit whether the sack is on or off. The first team to win ten points wins the game. Children can switch teams for playing another round.

**5. SPECIAL HINT:** This activity can be done with teams in quiz-show format. Make sure that everyone gets a turn.

# Word Search

**1. OBJECTIVES:** To learn that communicating information requires clear explanations and questions and careful listening. Specifically, to take turns giving directions and asking questions in order to locate the hidden words.

**2. RELATIONSHIP** to the development of empathy: Assuming the perspective of another by understanding the need for supplying missing information in communicating directions.

**3. MATERIALS:** "Word Search" for each child. (See p. 39.)

**4. PROCEDURE:** Have the children sit so as to avoid seeing anyone else's paper. Tell the children to search for the hidden words; then ask individuals to describe the location of a word he or she has found. Descriptions should be as accurate and complete as possible, and listeners should be encouraged to ask questions for clarification when necessary.

**5. SPECIAL HINTS:** Other word search pages can be used, and this activity can be repeated. To make it more difficult, do not list the words to be found on the page. This is usually a popular activity. The children may need to be reminded to focus on clear direction giving instead of hurrying to complete their pages independently.

# Tape Recordings I

**1. OBJECTIVES:** To learn that different emotions can be conveyed through varying tones of voice. Specifically, to tape record sentences in various tones of voice.

**2. RELATIONSHIP** to the development of empathy: Using auditory cues to discriminate affect; encouraging emotional responsiveness.

**3. MATERIALS:** Tape recorder and blank tapes.

**4. PROCEDURE:** Give the following examples of emotions conveyed through different tones of voice, and ask the children to identify the emotion or tone:

"Now, what will we do!" (angry)
"Now, what will we do?" (problem solving)
"Now, what will we do?" (whining)

Ask for other examples of sentences that show emotions, and have the children repeat the sentences in several different tones of voice. Then record each child, playing back the recording to the group after all have had turns. You might use: Go to bed. Help me. Is it hot? Are you finished? You want to go. What's that? What did you say?

**5. SPECIAL HINTS:** Children may have trouble thinking of more than two ways to say their sentences ("angry" and "normal"). You might help by describing circumstances that might cause sentences to be said in different ways, or you might describe various roles that might cause people to use different tones of voice. For example, "Go to bed," said by a tired, frustrated mother, by a mother or father telling a sick child what to do, by a new babysitter begging a little kid, or by an angry older brother to a younger child, and so forth.

# What Ifs
# and Mysteries

**1. OBJECTIVES:** To develop an understanding that people may have differing perspectives about the same situations, depending on their past experiences and feelings. Specifically, to offer and discuss various explanations for the actions of others.

**2. RELATIONSHIP** to the development of empathy: Interpreting social cues; assuming the perspective of another.

**3. MATERIALS:** "What Ifs" and "Mysteries" lists. (See pp. 40–41.)

**4. PROCEDURE A:** Discuss the idea that different people react differently to situations, and that there is usually a reason why people pick a particular solution or why they act the way they do. Read the "What Ifs" list, and ask the children to describe what the individual would do for each of the circumstances described. After discussing all of the examples, ask the children to act out the alternative behaviors. Ask children to think of "what if" examples of their own.

**PROCEDURE B:** Using the "Mysteries" list, ask the children to provide their own explanations of circumstances that might have caused the puzzling behavior. Encourage the children to offer as many alternatives as they can.

**5. SPECIAL HINTS:** The discussion should move as rapidly as possible; if interest lags, skip the more complicated examples. Generating personal examples may be difficult for children, but you might be able to help by offering some suggestions.

# Guided Walk

**1. OBJECTIVES:** To experience and discuss the differences of perspective required in giving and following directions. Specifically, to take turns in guiding and being guided around the room, with and without blindfolds.

**2. RELATIONSHIP** to the development of empathy: Assuming the perspective of another.

**3. MATERIALS:** Blindfolds.

**4. PROCEDURE A:** During the "Camera Walk" activity, the children discussed the physical setting of the room and tried visualizing it when they were not looking at it. Remind them of their experiences, the discussion, and of the "Camera Walk." For "Guided Walk," pairs of children take turns guiding a blindfolded partner around an obstacle course in the classroom. Guides should give verbal directions and walk about the room with their partner, but guides should try to avoid guiding physically. Emphasize trusting the guide, and giving good, clear, trustworthy directions. The children should switch roles, so everyone can be both guide and follower. You might ask: Which is the harder job, being guide or follower? Why? Is it hard to give directions?

**PROCEDURE B:** After the Guided Walk and discussion, the children should again work in pairs, one as "Master Controller" and one as "Robot." In this activity, the "Master Controller" tells the "Robot" what to do, as exactly and completely as possible. You may demonstrate with a volunteer. The "Controller" stays in one place and directs the "Robot" around the room. The children should switch roles, so everyone can be both "Master Controller" and "Robot." You might ask: Which is the harder job, being "Master Controller" or "Robot"? Why? Is it hard to follow directions when you disagree with what you have been told to do?

**5. SPECIAL HINT:** Remind the children to use the "stop" command if they get confused or if the "Robot" is headed for trouble.

# Late for Dinner—Was Dawn Right?

**1. OBJECTIVES:** To understand that individuals in a conflict situation may have differing perspectives and feelings. Specifically, to watch a film and role play alternative endings presented in the film.

**2. RELATIONSHIP** to the development of empathy: In order to discover the story line the children will need to discriminate the affect and body language of the characters. The children will be given practice in assuming the perspective and roles of the mother and daughter in the picture.

**3. MATERIALS:** The film "Late for Dinner—Was Dawn Right?" by Encyclopaedia Britannica (film #2995), film projector.

**4. PROCEDURE:** Advance the film past the title frames and do not tell the children the title of the movie. Show the film once with no sound, and ask the children to figure out what is going on by looking at the actions and facial expressions of the characters. Before reshowing, ask some of the children to share their ideas of what the story is about. Show the film again, with sound, and ask the children to discuss whether or not they figured out the story without the sound. Next, briefly discuss the conflict between Dawn and her mother, identifying each one's perspective. Ask for volunteers to role play the two perspectives for alternative solutions, encouraging the children to change perspective and play the role of the other character the second time around.

**5. SPECIAL HINTS:** Remember to keep the title of the film a secret at first and to advance the film past the title frames. Other films or parts of films can be used in this fashion, particularly films that show conflict. Showing the scenes without sound is a good way to let the children practice reading emotion through body and facial cues.

# 29

# Problem Stories I

**1. OBJECTIVES:** To develop alternative solutions to conflicts depicted in the vignettes. Specifically, to create puppets to role play characters in the vignettes.

**2. RELATIONSHIP** to the development of empathy: Assuming the perspective and role of another.

**3. MATERIALS:** List of vignettes (see p. 42), paper bags, felt, glue, scissors.

**4. PROCEDURE:** Pass out materials for making puppets, telling the children that their puppets will be used to finish some stories that do not have endings. When the children have finished making their puppets, they should listen to the three vignettes and discuss various alternatives for ending each story. Ask for volunteers to portray the characters in each vignette. The names and sexes of the characters can be changed to meet the needs of the puppets and children in your particular group. Once the children have acted out one solution to the situation, it is a good idea to ask them to change roles and act out the story again. For instance, if a teacher and a student are involved in one situation, encourage the children to play both roles with their puppets before another group of children takes their place.

**5. SPECIAL HINTS:** Ask for alternative solutions to the situations and encourage the children to play both roles. More than two children may get involved at one time. Ensure that the acting is centered on alternative solutions, rather than being a replay of what is given in the vignette.

# 30

# Can You Guess What Makes Me Feel?

**1. OBJECTIVES:** To understand that different situations may generate different emotional reactions in people. Specifically, to play a game in which the children guess the reasons for different emotional reactions.

**2. RELATIONSHIP** to the development of empathy: Assuming the perspective and role of another person; encouraging emotional responsiveness.

**3. MATERIALS:** List of emotion words from which the children generate possible reasons for the emotion. Children may help generate this list.

**4. PROCEDURE:** This game is similar to the game of 20 Questions in that children are to ask yes or no questions about what could have caused someone ("It") to feel happy, sad, and so forth. Start the exercise by listing emotional words (happy, sad, and so forth) on the board. Encourage the children to add words that they think should be included. Next, set the "theme" word for each round by announcing an emotion. For instance, you might indicate that for the first round, the children are to guess possible reasons why "It" feels happy. The children then ask yes or no questions to determine what caused "It" to feel the emotion chosen for that particular round. For instance, a child might ask, "Do you feel happy because someone did something nice for you?" or "Do you feel happy because you are doing something nice for someone else?" You should play the game too, to provide a demonstration of effective question-asking strategies. The winner of each round starts the next (gets to be "It"). Everyone should have a turn.

**5. SPECIAL HINTS:** This game provides an opportunity for children to think about personal emotion-causing situations as well as to learn about others. They should therefore be encouraged to think of personal examples rather than following the examples of others. This activity can be done at various times. To make it more complex, children should try to act out their guesses.

### *Emotion Words*

| | |
|---|---|
| Happy | Surprised |
| Sad | Curious |
| Angry | Worried |
| Afraid | Embarrassed |
| | Proud |

# Taking Group Pictures

**1.OBJECTIVES:** To increase the understanding that particular facial cues communicate information about particular affective states. Specifically, to photograph children portraying various emotions that are then identified and discussed.

**2.RELATIONSHIP** to the development of empathy: Discriminating and labeling the affective states in oneself and others; encouraging emotional responsiveness.

**3.MATERIALS:** Polaroid camera and film; list of emotionally charged situations, pictures of faces with varying emotional expressions.

**4.PROCEDURE:** Read a sentence describing an emotionally charged situation, and then photograph individuals as they act an emotion they might feel about the situation. Say: "Listen carefully to this story. When I stop reading, show how the person in the story would feel. Then I will take a picture." After all the children have been photographed, place the developed photos on a table and identify the emotional expressions portrayed. Try to match the photos with the sentences read earlier. Let each child mount a photo and record the appropriate sentence.

**5.SPECIAL HINTS:** Children might need some practice acting out the sentences before a picture is taken, or they might want to take turns thinking of their own sentences for the group to act out. The pictures can be used to decorate the room.

### Emotionally Charged Situations

1. You just get a new bike.
2. You're moving away.
3. Someone takes your pencil.
4. You are accused of breaking a glass.
5. You're lost.
6. Your dog was just hit by a car.
7. Your friend's grandfather just died.
8. Nobody wants to play with you.
9. You just got a great report card.
10. You get to go to the beach.
11. You have to stay home and work around the house.
12. You always get blamed for what your brother (sister) does.
13. You just broke a window.
14. You have to take a little kid with you to the show.
15. Your teacher just sent you to the principal's office.

# Recognizing and Explaining Incongruities

**1.OBJECTIVES:** To understand that differences of opinion may occur when someone does not take into account another's needs or experience. Specifically, to interpret cartoonlike situations depicting misunderstandings.

**2.RELATIONSHIP** to the development of empathy: Assuming the perspective of another.

**3.MATERIALS:** Cartoons depicting incongruities. (See pp. 43–53.)

**4.PROCEDURE:** Describe the cartoons as situations in which people are involved who do not fully understand what another wants or needs. The results are humorous. Say, "These pictures show people doing and thinking and talking about different things. In each cartoon one of the people has not thought carefully about something that the other people or person needs. The situations are funny because something was forgotten—it's our job now to figure out what the person talking or thinking or acting forgot about the other person—what makes the situation funny. In the first one, for example, the saleswoman is showing her customer a dress. She is saying, 'Here, try this one. It looks like just the right one for you.' What is the saleswoman forgetting?" (The customer is very thin, but the dress is very large.)

Introduce each cartoon, using the description of the scene. Be sure that all the children have a chance to offer explanations for the causes of various incongruous situations.

**5.SPECIAL HINTS:** Emphasize the lack of perspective taking as the cause for each incongruity. The children might want to try drawing their own incongruous situations. This could be set up as a workshop or center activity by providing a careful description of what makes the situation incongruous. You might want to cover the cartoons with plastic folders to make them easier to handle (and more resistant to handling.)

# 33
# Levels of Emotional Intensity

**1. OBJECTIVES:** To recognize degrees of intensity of the same emotion. Specifically, to discuss and act out situations that evoke varying degrees of emotional intensity.

**2. RELATIONSHIP** to the development of empathy: Discriminating and labeling affect; developing emotional responsiveness.

**3. MATERIALS:** Two decks of cards—one deck with names of emotions, the other with degrees of intensity. For example, *very, somewhat, a little,* and so forth.

**4. PROCEDURE A:** Begin by speaking in a soft whisper. Ask, "What am I doing?" Repeat the question with increasing volume, and lead a discussion about situations that cause people to whisper, shout, laugh hard, or cry, comparing them with situations that evoke a loud voice, a smile, or a sad face. Ask, "What do people do when they

1. are at football games?"
2. see an old friend after a long separation?"
3. win or lose a race?"
4. say goodbye to an old friend for a long separation?"
5. get all A's?"
6. realize that it's only five minutes to recess?"
7. see it's a cloudy day?"
8. come in second in a race?"
9. say goodbye to a friend who is going on vacation for a little while?"

Ask for examples of shouting for joy or anger, or of crying for joy or sorrow.

**PROCEDURE B:** Show the cards and explain that the children should take turns choosing one card from each pile and describing a situation that fits the cards they drew, while the other children identify the situation and guess what was written on the cards the "target" child selected.

**5. SPECIAL HINTS:** This exercise is designed to be a discussion and guessing game, but if children want to act out the situations, they should be encouraged to do so.

# 34
# Late Arriver*

**1. OBJECTIVES:** To understand that viewpoints depend on one's knowledge of a situation. Specifically, to listen to and discuss two stories in which the characters have different knowledge.

**2. RELATIONSHIP** to the development of empathy: Assuming the perspective of another; "de-centering."

**3. MATERIALS:** Story and cartoons for "Broken Window," Late-Arriver stories 1–5. (See pp. 54–64.)

**4. PROCEDURE A:** Show the cartoons for "Broken Window" and tell the story to the group. Ask the children to identify (1) what the owner of the house thinks and how he feels, (2) what the police think, and (3) what the children think and how they feel. The discussion should emphasize the *lack* of knowledge of the owner compared to the more extensive knowledge of the children.

**PROCEDURE B:** Select one volunteer to leave the room before reading the first story. Halfway through the story, recall the child and have him or her listen to the ending. The group who heard the entire story then tells only the part of the story that the latecomer heard, without including any extra details. The latecomer should confirm the group's accuracy. Ask the latecomer to explain the causes of the events. Ask, "Why did that happen?" Emphasize the latecomer's understanding of the event compared to the more extensive knowledge and understanding of the group who heard the entire story.

**5. SPECIAL HINTS:** This activity is like a game, and the children enjoy being the Late Arriver. It is important that they pay close attention to the stories and that they realize the need to think about rather than guess at the information. Be sure that all children can see the cartoons. They can "read" the story from the pictures.

*Adapted from M. Chandler, "Egocentrism and Antisocial Behavior: The Assessment and Training of Social Perspective Taking Skills," *Developmental Psychology* 9 (1973): 326–332.

# 35

# Tape Recordings II

**1. OBJECTIVES:** To learn that feelings can be conveyed through tone of voice. Specifically, to create and listen to tape recordings of nonsense syllables that express different feelings through tone of voice.

**2. RELATIONSHIP** to the development of empathy: Labeling affect; discriminating affect auditorily; encouraging emotional responsiveness.

**3. MATERIALS:** Tape recorded "conversations" of nonsense syllables spoken with changes in tone of voice implying different emotions. Blank tape for children to make their own recordings.

**4. PROCEDURE:** Introduce the concept of tone of voice. Lead a discussion giving your own examples as well as eliciting examples from the group concerning phrases or situations in which the speaker's tone of voice conveys a message or feeling. Say, "Can you think of a time when you knew what a person was saying more from his or her tone of voice than from the words?" Then play each prerecorded "conversation" of nonsense syllables and ask the children to think how each speaker feels in the situations. Focus especially on the cues that indicate, for example, that "the man is angry" or "the woman is scared." Play tapes as many times as necessary for children to "hear" the feelings. Encourage the children to invent their own nonsense syllables. (You may need to offer suggestions.) Children should practice their "words" to themselves to become familiar with them before trying to record them. Listing animals, colors, or numbers instead of nonsense syllables may be easier. For example, in angry or happy tones, they may say "red, yellow, blue green." Children should then choose an emotion and try to convey it through their tone of voice. Record each child's voice, and play it back when all have been recorded, so the group can identify the emotion through the tone of voice.

**5. SPECIAL HINTS:** "Nonsense syllables" may be a confusing idea to the children. Emphasize that words or syllables are often not as important as tone of voice in conveying information.

# 36

# Rufus

**1. OBJECTIVES:** To understand that there may be more than one perspective in a given situation, depending on the knowledge of the various characters involved. Specifically, to listen to and discuss a story in which the characters hold two different perspectives.

**2. RELATIONSHIP** to the development of empathy: Assuming the perspectives of another.

**3. MATERIALS:** "Rufus" story. (See p. 65.)

**4. PROCEDURE:** Read "Rufus." Then lead a discussion focusing on the reasons for Andy's behavior and his comments to Rufus. Encourage the children to suggest and role play different endings to the vignette. Ask them to think of experiences of their own that are similar to those of Rufus.

**5. SPECIAL HINTS:** In this activity the children, as audience, are privy to more information than any character in the story. Individuals rarely have access to such knowledge, but one can often infer much from others' behaviors. Encourage the children to think of times when they knew more than they were told and could understand another's perspective by thinking about what the other person knew.

# Tape Recording with a Partner

**1. OBJECTIVES:** To develop interpersonal communication skills. Specifically, to listen to and repeat another child's verbal presentation.

**2. RELATIONSHIP** to the development of empathy: Before discriminating the affective states of another, it is necessary for children to pay close attention to and communicate with others.

**3. MATERIALS:** Stopwatch with a second hand.

**4. PROCEDURE:** Ask for a volunteer and demonstrate one episode, playing both roles, before the children try it by themselves. Ask the children to form pairs and sit facing each other, paying very close attention to their partners and ignoring the other children. One student in each pair begins when you signal. He or she talks for ten seconds on ONLY the topic you provide (see list). At the end of ten seconds, the partner tries to repeat as much as he or she can remember. After the repetition, the first child fills in anything that was left out. Partners should then change roles, and the second member of the pair should speak for ten seconds. Repeat the above process. Increase the time to twenty seconds and follow the same procedure. If the children are "into" this, increase the time even more. If not, discuss how it felt when the other child didn't remember something that one member of the pair had said. Finally, discuss how it felt when they themselves couldn't remember what someone else said.

**5. SPECIAL HINTS:** Remember to have the children "fill in" what the other child forgot. Try to ask questions that emphasize the difference between the talking and listening positions, when it seems appropriate. You might use the following topics:

Where would you like to visit?

What is your favorite holiday and what do you like to do on that holiday?

What would you do if you could do anything you wanted?

What would you use a magic wish for?

Once when I was scared I . . .

Something I am proud of is . . .

Something that makes me really angry is . . .

Something that made me laugh is . . .

What is your favorite food?

What are your favorite television shows?

What is your favorite game?

# Problem Stories II

**1. OBJECTIVES:** To enhance role-playing skills. Specifically, to role play different characters and to develop alternative solutions to conflicts depicted in the vignettes.

**2. RELATIONSHIP** to the development of empathy: Assuming the role of another person.

**3. MATERIALS:** List of vignettes (see p. 66) and props provided for the children to use.

**4. PROCEDURE:** Have the children form a circle about six feet across. Say, "The stories for today are short, and they do not end. They are not finished. Our job is to try to think of some ways to end them. When someone has an idea, we will act it out and see what happens. There are lots of ways to finish each story." Then read Vignette 1 and hold a brief discussion regarding different ways of ending the story. It is important to stress generating alternative solutions. After a brief discussion, ask for volunteers to act out one of the solutions mentioned previously. The names and or sexes of the characters in the vignettes can be changed to meet the needs of the children in the particular group. After the children have acted out one solution to the situation, it is a good idea to ask them to change roles and act out the story again. For instance, if a teacher and a student are involved in one situation, encourage the children to play both roles before another group of children takes their place. Handle vignettes 2, 3, and 4 in the same way.

**5. SPECIAL HINTS:** Ask for alternative solutions to the situations and encourage the children to play both roles in the vignettes. More than two children may get involved at one time. Puppets may be used instead of having the children act.

# Step-by-Step Perspective Drawing

**1. OBJECTIVES:** To understand that one's visual perspective of objects depends on one's location. Specifically, to have the children draw a picture of an object from their own and another's perspective.

**2. RELATIONSHIP** to the development of empathy: Understanding and assuming the perspective of another.

**3. MATERIALS:** Drawing paper; pencils; erasers; three nonsymmetrical objects, for example, a cup, small saucepan, and building blocks of different geometric shapes.

**4. PROCEDURE A:** Tell the children that they are going to draw a picture one step at a time. Be sure they are spread out around a table so that they can all see the objects placed in the middle, but from different perspectives. Begin by placing one object in the center, and tell the children to draw it exactly as it looks to them. Help them to show depth and angles as carefully as possible. When all have drawn the first object, have them share their pictures and discuss why they look different. For example, the handle might be on the opposite side of the cup, or not visible at all. Then add a second object and ask children to draw it. For some children, the addition will block part of the original object, and they will have to erase part of their first drawing. When all have drawn the second object, discuss the differences and the reasons for the differences in their pictures. Add a third object, and proceed as before.

**PROCEDURE B:** Have each child sit directly across from another, and tell the children that they are going to draw the picture that their partner sees. They may ask questions such as, "Can you see the handle on the right?" But they should be encouraged to stay in their seats and to avoid moving. When they are finished, the partners should trade pictures and verify the views.

**5. SPECIAL HINTS:** Perspective drawing is a difficult task, and children may need individual help. Accuracy is important only in terms of angles and spacing not in terms of perfect representation.

# Story Excerpt

**1. OBJECTIVES:** To experience and understand an emotional response to a predetermined story selection. Specifically, to listen to story excerpts presenting emotionally arousing situations in order to discuss reactions to the stories.

**2. RELATIONSHIP** to the development of empathy: Emotional responsiveness.

**3. MATERIALS:** Story excerpt from *A Tree Grows in Brooklyn* (New York: Harper & Row, 1943) by Betty Smith. (See pp. 67–68.)

**4. PROCEDURE:** Tell the children you have a story about children who are close to their age. The story is about a girl and her younger brother the summer before they start school.

Read the excerpt. Then ask each child to think carefully about, and possibly write down, the answer to: "How does that make you feel?" Then ask each child to tell his or her answer, and discuss why they have various feelings. Be sure to clarify any comprehension questions. Also, help children understand the reasons that caused them to feel certain emotions. There is no "right" answer, and sometimes children will have interesting reasons for responses that are significantly different from everyone else's.

**5. SPECIAL HINTS:** Be sure to emphasize that there is no right or wrong answer. This is *not* a test. If you feel that comprehension may be a problem for your children, give more of an introduction to the story.

# Blank Pages

**1. OBJECTIVES:** To learn that communicating information requires clear explanations and questions and careful listening. Specifically, to take turns giving directions and asking questions in order to complete a ditto.

**2. RELATIONSHIP** to the development of empathy: Assuming the perspective of another by understanding the need for supplying missing information in communicating directions.

**3. MATERIALS:** Crayons or felt pens, blank paper.

**4. PROCEDURE:** Have the children sit in a large circle facing out, with writing boards or books on their laps or on the floor. Ask one child at a time to give directions to the group, describing a part of a picture or design to be drawn. For example, "Draw a two-inch red square in the top right hand corner." Listeners must ask specific questions to clarify the directions. The children should avoid looking at each other's pictures until the end of the activity. When the drawings are completed, have the children compare their pictures to see how successful they were. You might ask: Was it easier to give directions or to follow directions? What was hard about it?

**5. SPECIAL HINTS:** It is important to encourage the children to ask questions if they do not understand the directions given. You might help by giving examples of effective directions and questions. If the group is having difficulty, it helps to begin a drawing of your own, on the blackboard or on tagboard, following the directions given by the children. Use your picture only as a "check" on your own work.

# Pick a Present for Your Partner

1. **OBJECTIVES:** To increase perspective taking. Specifically, to play a game in which the children anticipate what another person would like for a gift.

2. **RELATIONSHIP** to the development of empathy: Assuming the perspective of another.

3. **MATERIALS:** Display board with a variety of pictures of gifts.

4. **PROCEDURE:** *Part 1*   Have the children study the display; then have each child write down the name of the gift that he or she would most like to have. Collect the papers. Then instruct the children to write down the gifts that they think the other group members chose for themselves. They should not talk to each other about their choices. Collect these papers as well.

*Part 2*   After all papers have been collected, discuss whether or not and why each child feels that the particular gift or gifts chosen for him or her were appropriate.

5. **SPECIAL HINTS:** The children should not talk to each other until all gift selections have been made. In leading the discussion in Part 2, first go around the circle of children asking them which gift they think a particular child would want. After all the children have had a turn to respond, check with the child to find out which gift he or she actually requested. Repeat this sequence for all children in the group. This exercise can be used with hypothetical gifts, in which case the selections might be expensive or exotic, or with less expensive presents that may actually be given to the children. Choices should include as many non-sex-stereotyped items as possible.

# Emotions in a Hat

1. **OBJECTIVES:** To gain a greater understanding of the relationship between certain situations and affective reactions. Specifically, to act out and guess situations suggested by others in the group.

2. **RELATIONSHIP** to the development of empathy: Emotional responsiveness; assuming the role of another.

3. **MATERIALS:** Small slips of paper; pencils; hat.

4. **PROCEDURE:** Say "Today we are going to think of situations that make you proud or angry." Ask if someone can think of a situation that made him or her proud. Next, ask if someone can think of a situation that made him or her angry. Discuss a few situations that are volunteered. Then choose a child to act out one of the suggested reasons for feeling proud. The other children should guess the circumstances and situation being acted out. Repeat the process for "angry." After the children have had the opportunity to act out their own reasons for feeling proud or angry, pass out paper and pencils and tell the children to write down a situation that would or has made them feel proud. Collect the slips and put them in a hat. Then have the children take turns choosing slips of paper from the hat and acting out the situation portrayed so that the other children may guess. Repeat this process for "angry."

5. **SPECIAL HINTS:** The children should not act out the situations they have contributed or guess while someone else is acting it out. Acting out situations may be difficult for some children. Puppets made in a previous exercise may be used if children are uncomfortable about acting out.

# 44

# Problem Stories III

**1. OBJECTIVES:** To enhance role-playing skills. Specifically, to role play different characters and to develop alternative solutions to conflicts.

**2. RELATIONSHIP** to the development of empathy: Assuming the perspective and role of another.

**3. MATERIALS:** List of problem stories (see p. 69) and puppets that the children made previously.

**4. PROCEDURE:** Have the children form a circle about six feet across. Say, "The stories for today are short, and they have no endings; they are not finished. Our job is to think of some ways to end them. When someone has an idea, we will act it out and see what happens. There are lots of ways to finish each story." Then read the first problem story and hold a brief discussion regarding different ways of ending it. It is important to stress generating alternative solutions. After a brief discussion, ask for volunteers to act out one of the solutions previously discussed. The names and/or sexes of the characters can be changed to meet the needs of the children in your particular group. Once the children have acted out one solution to the situation, it is a good idea to ask them to change roles and act out the story again. For instance, if a teacher and a student are involved in one situation, encourage the children to play both roles before another group of children takes their place.

**5. SPECIAL HINTS:** It is necessary to ask for alternative solutions to the situations and to encourage the children to play both roles.

# WORKSHEETS

WORKSHEETS

NAME: _____

From *Learning to Care.* Copyright © 1983 Scott, Foresman and Company.

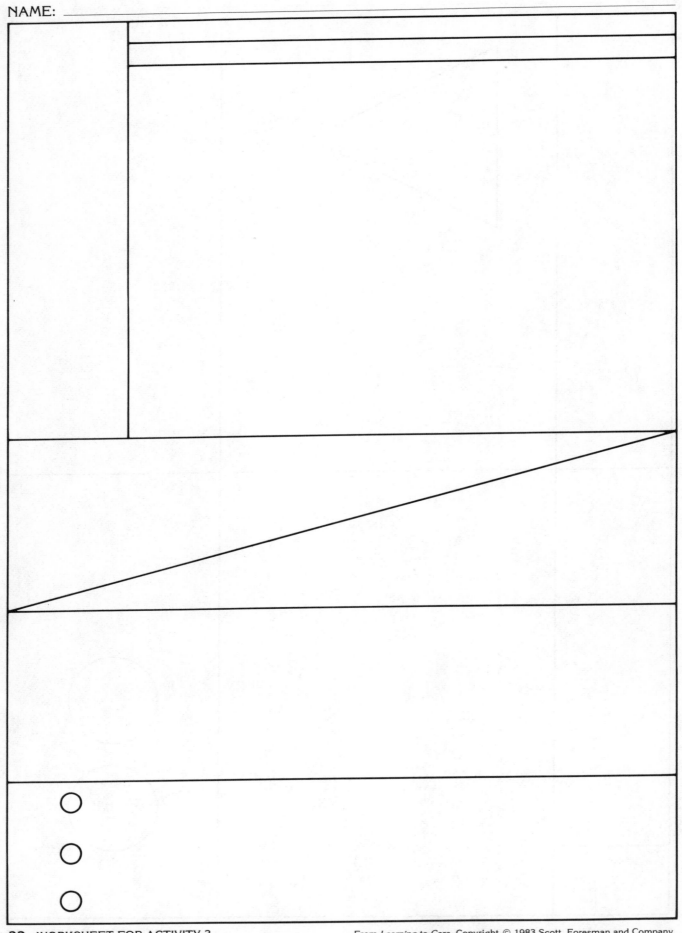

From *Learning to Care.* Copyright © 1983 Scott, Foresman and Company.

From *Learning to Care.* Copyright © 1983 Scott, Foresman and Company.

NAME:

From *Learning to Care*. Copyright © 1983 Scott, Foresman and Company.

From *Learning to Care*. Copyright © 1983 Scott, Foresman and Company.

NAME: _____

# Joey

**Version 1:** Joey loves to play ball, but he is not allowed to throw the ball in the house. His older brother, Robert, is babysitting one day because their mother has to work on Saturday to pay the bills (the family is very poor). Joey has a big game coming up soon, but because it's raining outside, he practices pitching into the couch. Everything is fine for a long time, until the ball bounces off the edge of the couch and through a window. His older brother wakes up, and their mother arrives home from work.

**Version 2:** Joey's mother, Mrs. Johnson, had to get up early Saturday morning to go to work. She hates to leave the kids alone all day but she has no choice; she has to do *something* to get money for the bills. While she's at work she finds herself daydreaming about her sons whenever she has a free moment. She worries about them from time to time but reassures herself that Joey's brother is old enough to look after the two of them. And because it's raining, she thinks they are probably both quietly reading. At last the end of the day comes, and she can go home and relax. When she walks up the front stairs she sees the broken window.

**Version 3:** Joey's brother, Robert, spends many of his Saturdays watching Joey, and he's tired of it. Besides, Joey hardly needs to be watched at all; he never gets into trouble. This Saturday it is raining and Robert is tired, so he stretches out on the bed for awhile to rest. The next thing he hears is the sound of breaking glass. He opens his eyes, and just as he is getting up to see what has happened, his mother walks through the door.

  From *Learning to Care.* Copyright © 1983 Scott, Foresman and Company.

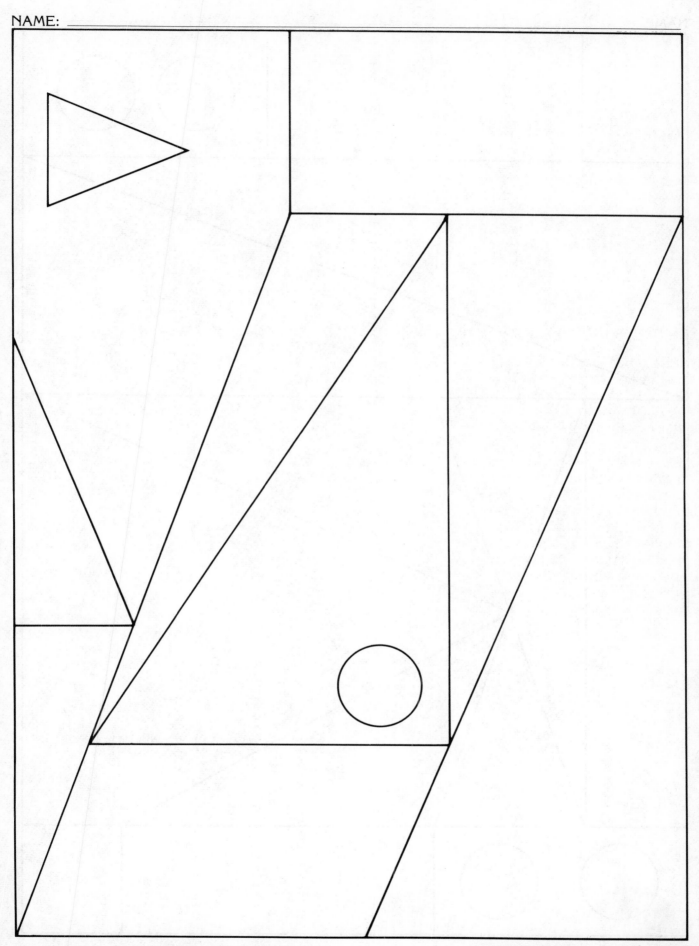

From *Learning to Care.* Copyright © 1983 Scott, Foresman and Company.

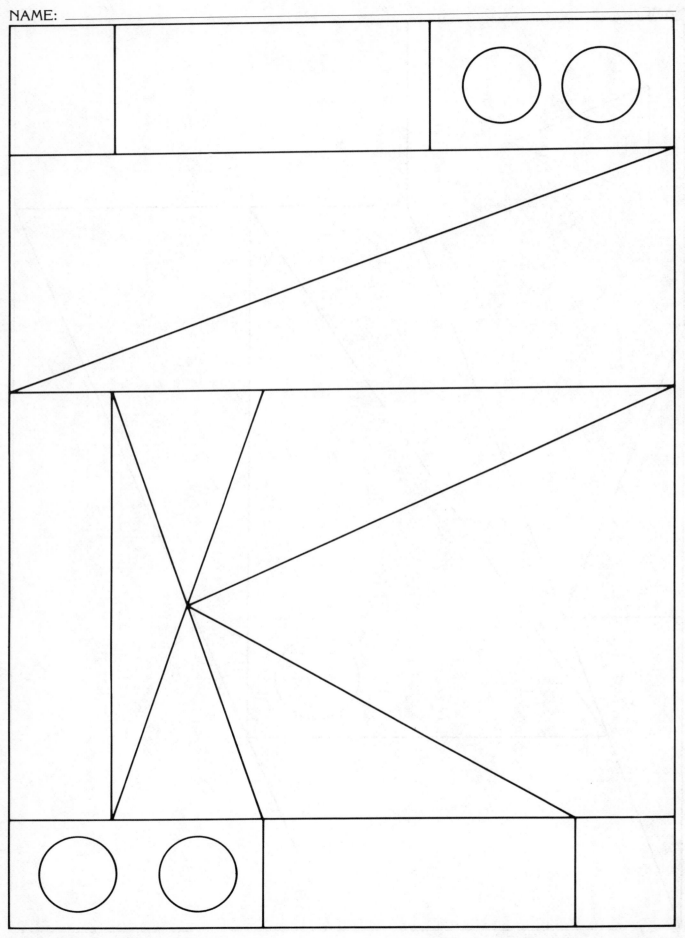

From *Learning to Care.* Copyright © 1983 Scott, Foresman and Company.

# Word Search

In the puzzle below, find words by reading: **Forward,** from left to right (like the word *RED*) **Down,** from top to bottom (like the word *YELLOW*) **Diagonally,** on a slant from top to bottom or from left to right (like the word *GREEN*)

First, study the list of colors, then find the color words in the puzzle and circle them. After you find a word, cross it off the list. Cross off the words that have been found for you.

TAN
RED
BLUE
PINK
GRAY
GOLD
BROWN
BLACK
GREEN
PURPLE
YELLOW
SILVER

| L | S | P | I | N | K | P | Z | R | Q | M | O | Y |
|---|---|---|---|---|---|---|---|---|---|---|---|---|
| V | O | I | Z | K | B | V | T | J | O | N | T | E |
| L | M | B | L | U | E | Z | O | V | M | B | C | L |
| X | Y | L | C | V | D | V | Q | W | G | R | T | L |
| P | B | V | O | L | E | M | N | D | J | K | Z | O |
| V | M | N | B | R | S | R | E | D | T | G | H | W |
| G | L | M | N | P | O | Z | X | G | M | N | O | P |
| L | O | V | M | N | Z | G | R | B | R | O | W | N |
| G | H | L | M | N | B | C | A | L | L | E | M | O |
| Z | V | B | D | O | T | T | L | A | M | A | E | Z |
| B | D | O | L | G | R | A | Y | C | Q | R | M | N |
| Y | O | P | L | Z | V | N | A | K | R | B | O | B |
| H | E | P | U | R | P | L | E | S | O | N | D | E |

From *Learning to Care*. Copyright © 1983 Scott, Foresman and Company.

# What If . . .

1. a dog who is held on a leash by its owner approaches
   a. a child who has been seriously injured by a dog bite?
   b. a child who has never had a bad experience with dogs?
2. a family buys a brand new piano and
   a. the daughter loves music and loves to play all musical instruments?
   b. the mother always nags the daughter to practice. The daughter plays badly and has never managed to produce a nice sound from any instrument?
3. it is raining too hard to play outside and
   a. a child loves to sit and read for hours?
   b. a child hates to sit still but loves to ride bicycles and play sports?
4. a teacher scolds
   a. a child who gets scolded all the time?
   b. a child who never gets in trouble and is almost never scolded?
5. a child drops his notebook, and all the papers fly out all over the floor?
   a. The child is having a good day and feels happy.
   b. The child has had one bad thing happen after another all day.
6. a child accidentally spills water on a painting she had almost finished?
   a. She has always been very neat and tidy and likes to have everything "just right."
   b. She likes to use paint spills to make designs on the painting.
7. a boy tears his shirt while playing ball?
   a. His mother is very strict and is very fussy about her children's clothing.
   b. His mother laughs at small problems and does not become upset easily.

  From *Learning to Care.* Copyright © 1983 Scott, Foresman and Company.

# Mysteries

1. A girl wears long sleeves when it is 100 degrees outside.
2. Billy opens the door to his classroom and sits down in his seat just before the first bell rings. Everyone turns and stares at him in surprise.
3. Sally walks into her house after school and finds her mother working in the kitchen. "Hi, Mom," she says. Her mother blows up at her in anger.
4. William and Jose are good friends. But one day, Jose starts acting "funny." He runs right past William on the playground at recess, and he doesn't even turn around when William calls to him. All during recess and after school, Jose doesn't talk to William.
5. Jim is asked to stay after school by his teacher, who tells him she knows that he took some money from her desk. Jim is glad she caught him.

6. During a movie about a child whose dog runs away and gets lost, a woman in the audience starts to cry.
7. The teacher says that anyone who doesn't have lunch money on the first day of school can borrow money from the office. Jane has no lunch money, but she doesn't go the office to borrow.
8. Charles drops his pencil by accident during class. His teacher becomes furious and sends him to the principal's office.
9. Mrs. Smith is insulted when a new acquaintance begins explaining different kinds of Mexican food to her.
10. Maria isn't interested in wearing makeup, and she knows that her mother doesn't allow girls in the family to wear any until eighth grade. One day, she sneaks into her older sister's room and puts some lipstick and other makeup into her pocket.

From *Learning to Care.* Copyright © 1983 Scott, Foresman and Company.

# Problems

**l.** Laura borrows a sweater from Sally, promising to take good care of it. But when Laura returns the sweater, there is a big hole in it. Discuss with the children what to do about this. Encourage them to generate several alternatives to this conflict situation and to take turns playing both Laura and Sally.

**2.** Andrew must stay home and babysit for a younger sibling, and Paul is having a birthday party. Andrew had planned for a long time to go to the birthday party, but on the day of the party, his mother called up and said that she had to work late, so he couldn't go. Andrew really hates to miss the party and has even bought a gift. Paul calls to say that everyone is there and they are having a great time. Paul insists that Andrew leave the baby alone for just a little while and come over to the party. What will happen?

**3.** David never gets anywhere on time, and Jonathan must explain to the slowpoke that it's important to be on time. How can Jonathan explain to David that it's necessary to be on time?

   From *Learning to Care*. Copyright © 1983 Scott, Foresman and Company.

The thin woman wants to buy a new dress. The saleslady is saying to her, "Here, try this one. It looks like just the right one for you." What is the saleslady forgetting?

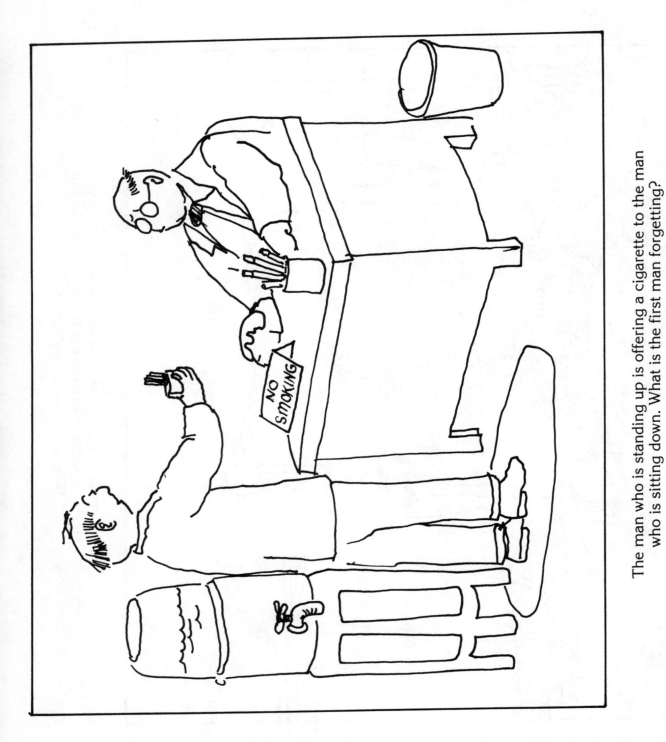

The man who is standing up is offering a cigarette to the man who is sitting down. What is the first man forgetting?

From *Learning to Care*. Copyright © 1983 Scott, Foresman and Company.

The man and the woman are doing different things in the picture. What is different about what they are doing? What are they forgetting?

From *Learning to Care.* Copyright © 1983 Scott, Foresman and Company.

The man next to the car wants to take these people to the airport.
What is he forgetting?

 From *Learning to Care*. Copyright © 1983 Scott, Foresman and Company.

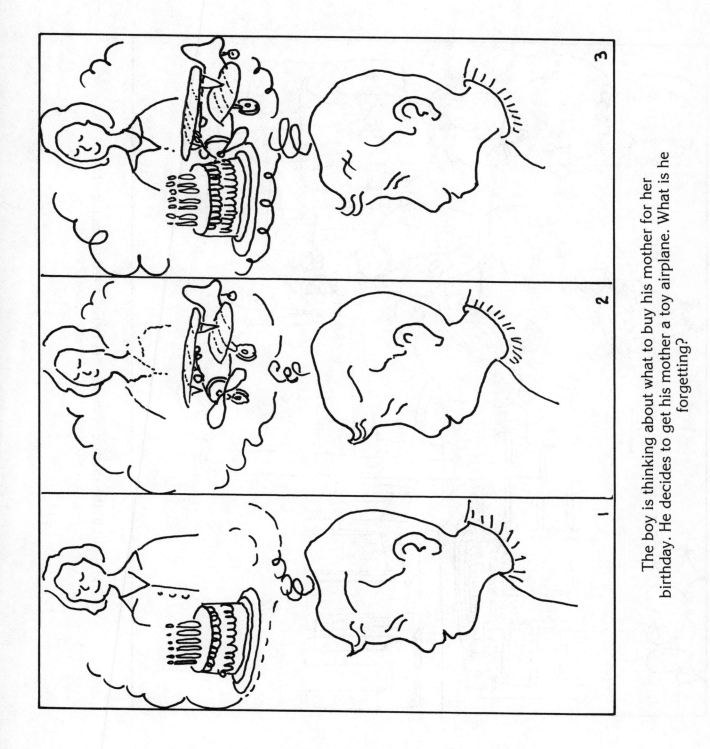

The boy is thinking about what to buy his mother for her birthday. He decides to get his mother a toy airplane. What is he forgetting?

From *Learning to Care.* Copyright © 1983 Scott, Foresman and Company.

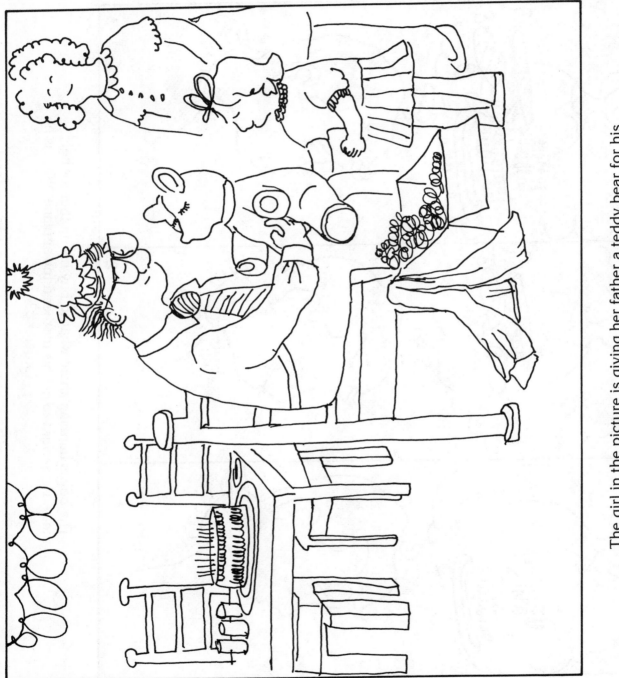

The girl in the picture is giving her father a teddy bear for his birthday. What did she forget?

From *Learning to Care.* Copyright © 1983 Scott, Foresman and Company.

The tall man is saying, "What do you think made this hole in the ground, anyway?" What is the tall man forgetting?

From *Learning to Care.* Copyright © 1983 Scott, Foresman and Company.

This man works at a donut shop all day. When he gets home, his wife offers him some donuts for a snack. What is the wife forgetting?

From *Learning to Care.* Copyright © 1983 Scott, Foresman and Company.

This boy is opening presents at his birthday party. All the presents are the same. What did his friends forget?

From *Learning to Care.* Copyright © 1983 Scott, Foresman and Company.  WORKSHEET FOR ACTIVITY 32  **51**

This girl is giving directions to a stranger. She tells him, "Well, go down to Tom's house and turn right." What is she forgetting?

From *Learning to Care.* Copyright © 1983 Scott, Foresman and Company.

This mother is saying to her children, "Don't play here in this mess. You might get dirty." What is the mother forgetting?

From *Learning to Care.* Copyright © 1983 Scott, Foresman and Company.

# Broken Window

A group of children is playing ball in the street. Their ball accidentally breaks a neighbor's window. The children run to the window to look over the damage. They ring the front doorbell, but no one answers. They remember that the man who lives there usually doesn't get home from work until 6 p.m. One boy says, "That gives us 2 hours to get the money together to pay for a new window. Let's split up and meet back here at 6 p.m. with as much money as we can get together." The children run off.

The owner of the house drives into his driveway earlier than usual. He is furious when he sees the broken window. He calls the police to investigate. The police arrive just as the boys come back to the house. In the last scene, the owner of the broken window is pointing angrily to the approaching boys.

  From *Learning to Care.* Copyright © 1983 Scott, Foresman and Company.

NAME: _____

From *Learning to Care*. Copyright © 1983 Scott, Foresman and Company.

NAME: _____

From *Learning to Care.* Copyright © 1983 Scott, Foresman and Company.

From *Learning to Care.* Copyright © 1983 Scott, Foresman and Company.

From *Learning to Care.* Copyright © 1983 Scott, Foresman and Company.

From *Learning to Care.* Copyright © 1983 Scott, Foresman and Company.

# Late Arriver 1

Tony is playing in the sandbox. The sand is nice and damp and easy to build with. He is building a sand castle that is tall and strong and better than any he's ever made before. He's very proud of it. He stands back to admire it. Just then Margaret comes screeching through the playground on her bike and knocks over the sand castle. It smashes all over the ground, but she keeps right on going.

Tony is furious. He's so angry he almost cries. He leaves the playground and goes home, still very angry.

**Enter Late Arriver**

Tony walks into the house and sees his baby brother, Larry, sitting on the floor playing with some cards. Larry has made his cards into a house that is even taller than he is, and he is very proud of it. Tony walks over to the card house and with one big breath, blows it down, scattering cards everywhere. Then he stomps out of the room. Larry is left sitting in the middle of the floor, wondering why Tony wrecked the card house.

 From *Learning to Care*. Copyright © 1983 Scott, Foresman and Company.

# Late Arriver 2

Yolanda planted a carrot in her garden. She waters it every day, pulls the weeds, and makes sure that nothing blocks the sun. She takes very good care of it. It grows and grows. All she can see is the green top, but she knows that it is healthy.

One day as she is coming home from school, she sees the biggest dog in the neighborhood digging in her yard. As she gets closer she sees that he has dug up her carrot and chewed it to shreds. Yolanda is heartbroken and almost starts to cry. She was so proud of that carrot, and now it is ruined.

**Enter Late Arriver**

Yolanda carries her school books into the house and goes into the bedroom. She stays in the room until her mother calls her for dinner. The family sits down to a dinner of chicken, rice, and carrots. Yolanda starts to cry, and the rest of the family wonders what is wrong.

# Late Arriver 3

Susie's mother gets up early to get Susie off to school on time every morning. Today as Susie is leaving for school her mother says, "I'm not feeling well today, Susie. I'm afraid I'm getting a cold. I'll probably be asleep when you get home from school, so please be quiet when you come in."

Susie's mother is an artist, and she paints lovely pictures. Their house is filled with her paintings. She has sent one special painting to a gallery to be sold, and she is waiting to hear whether anyone has bought it.

Later that day, Mrs. Brown wakes up from a nap and finds a letter from the gallery, telling her that her painting has been sold for a high price. Susie's mother is thrilled. She forgets about feeling sick, and she plans a big celebration for that night.

**Enter Late Arriver**

Susie is just getting home from school. She tiptoes into the house, and creeps into the kitchen. To her surprise, there is her mother, cooking up a storm, with a big smile on her face. Susie says, "Mom, you shouldn't be doing that."

From *Learning to Care.* Copyright © 1983 Scott, Foresman and Company.

NAME: _____

# Late Arriver 4

James and Francie decide to play a trick on Leslie on the way home from school. James has a squishy rubber spider in his pocket that looks very real and very scary. James and Francie run ahead of Leslie and hide behind a bush. When Leslie passes their hiding place on her way home, James and Francie both jump out and shake the spider in her face. Leslie screams and runs all the way home. James and Francie burst out laughing; they never saw anything so funny!

**Enter Late Arriver**

When James and Francie get home from school, they go out to play with their friends. After a while their father calls them in for supper. As they are helping to put things out on the table, their father notices a big spider in the corner of the room. He's busy, so he asks, "Francie, please kill that spider." James and Francie burst out laughing, and their parents look at them with surprise.

From *Learning to Care*. Copyright © 1983 Scott, Foresman and Company.

# Late Arriver 5

Mr. Allen is a bus driver and has been with the same company for five years. One day, at the end of his shift, his supervisor calls him in. "Nate," he says, "I've got good news for you. Your raise came through today. It's the big one—the one you've been hoping for. I'm glad; you deserve it." Mr. Allen is really happy. He smiles to himself as he walks home.

**Enter Late Arriver**

Mr. Allen and his son Peter are watching television after dinner. Peter is very nervous because he has to tell his father the sad thing that happened on his way home from school. While trying to do a wheelie on his bike, he skidded and popped a tire. He knows his father is going to be really mad, because earlier that week his father had caught him doing the same thing and had yelled at him. "Peter," he had said, "you know we don't have money to throw around for a new bicycle."

Peter works up his courage and finally tells his Dad about it. Peter is surprised to hear his father say, "Well, that's okay. We'll just have to buy you a new one."

   From *Learning to Care.* Copyright © 1983 Scott, Foresman and Company.

# Rufus

Rufus has a new ball that he just got for Christmas. He can't wait to go to the park and try it out. When he gets there, he sees his friend James, who is a little bit older than Rufus. Rufus decides to ask James if he wants to play ball with him, but before he asks him, James and a couple other big guys come over and take the ball away, saying, "Hey, now we've got a ball. Let's get a game up." At first Rufus is pleased, but then he realizes what is going to happen. James says, "No, you can't play. You're too little, and we've got enough *big* guys to play." Rufus is furious and starts yelling at James. James pushes Rufus off the court and tells him to leave them alone.

Rufus is really angry, but the other guys are bigger than he is, and he knows there is nothing he can do. Just then, Rufus' friend Andy comes by and thinks to himself, "That baby Rufus never wants to play. Look at him just moping by the side of the court." Andy calls out, "Hey Rufus, you turkey, how come you never want to play? What are you doin', just sittin' here? You always hang around, but you never want to get in a game."

From *Learning to Care.* Copyright © 1983 Scott, Foresman and Company.

# Problems

**1.** This situation involves two children, an older sister and a younger sister. The older sister has always been good to the younger sister, doing things like helping with homework, cleaning up, mowing the lawn, and so forth. But now she wants the younger sister to hide a puppy in the kitchen so that their parents won't find it. The younger sister doesn't want to say "no," but she doesn't want to do something that would make their parents mad. What can they do?

**2.** A brother and sister want to watch two different television shows. They have an argument over which show they should watch. What can they do?

**3.** Wayne lets Sarah borrow his favorite toy. Sarah accidentally loses the toy, and Wayne is angry. They are arguing about what they should do about the lost toy. What can they do?

**4.** This situation involves two characters, a student named Michael and the school principal. Michael knows who started a fire in the school but he doesn't want to tell the principal because the child who started the fire is one of his best friends. Should he tell the principal?

   From *Learning to Care.* Copyright © 1983 Scott, Foresman and Company.

# A Tree Grows in Brooklyn

**B. Smith**                                          **Harper & Row, 1943**

Francie was seven and Neeley six. Katie had held Francie back wishing both children to enter school together so that they could protect each other against the older children. On a dreadful Saturday in August, she stopped in the bedroom to speak to them before she went off to work. She awakened them and gave instructions.

"Now when you get up, wash yourselves good and when it gets to be eleven o'clock, go around the corner to the public health place, tell them to vaccinate you because you're going to school in September."

Francie began to tremble. Neeley burst into tears.

"You coming with us, Mama?" Francie pleaded.

"I've got to go to work. Who's going to do my work if I don't?" asked Katie covering up her conscience with indignation.

Francie said nothing more. Katie knew that she was letting them down. But she couldn't help it, she just couldn't help it. Yes, she should go with them to lend the comfort and authority of her presence but she knew she couldn't stand the ordeal. Yet, they had to be vaccinated. Her being with them or somewhere else couldn't take that fact away. So why shouldn't one of the three be spared? Besides, she said to her conscience, it's a hard and bitter world. They've got to live in it. Let them get hardened young to take care of themselves.

"Papa's going with us then," said Francie hopefully.

"Papa's at Headquarters waiting for a job. He won't be home all day. You're big enough to go alone. Besides, it won't hurt."

Neeley wailed on a higher key. Katie could hardly stand that. She loved the boy so much. Part of her reason for not going with them was that she couldn't bear to see the boy hurt . . . not even by a pin prick. Almost she decided to go with them. But no. If she went she'd lose half a day's work and she'd have to make it up on Sunday morning. Besides, she'd be sick afterwards. They'd manage somehow without her. She hurried off to her work.

Francie tried to console the terrified Neeley. Some older boys had told him that they cut your arm off when they got you in the Health Center. To take his mind off the thing, Francie took him down into the yard and they made mud pies. They quite forgot to wash as mama had told them to.

They almost forgot about eleven o'clock, the mud pie making was so beguiling. Their hands and arms got very dirty playing in the mud. At ten to eleven, Mrs. Gaddis hung out the window and yelled down that their mother had told her to remind them when it was near eleven o'clock. Neeley finished off his last mud pie, watering it with his tears. Francie took his hand and with slow dragging steps the children walked around the corner.

They took their place on a bench. Next to them sat a Jewish mama who clutched a large six-year-old boy in her arms and wept and kissed his forehead passionately from time to time. Other mothers sat there with grim suffering furrowed on their faces. Behind the frosted glass door where the terrifying business was going on, there was a steady bawling punctuated by a shrill scream, resumption of the bawling and then a pale child would come out with a strip of pure white gauze about his left arm. His

*Excerpt from pp. 129–132 in A TREE GROWS IN BROOKLYN by Betty Smith. Copyright 1943 by Betty Smith. Reprinted by permission of Harper & Row, Publishers, Inc.

From *Learning to Care.* Copyright © 1983 Scott, Foresman and Company.

mother would rush and grab him and with a foreign curse and a shaken fist at the frosted door, hurry him out of the torture chamber.

Francie went in trembling. She had never seen a doctor or a nurse in all of her small life. The whiteness of the uniforms, the shiny cruel instruments laid out on a napkin on a tray, the smell of antiseptics, and especially the cloudy sterilizer with its bloody red cross filled her with tongue-tied fright.

The nurse pulled up her sleeve and swabbed a spot clean on her left arm. Francie saw the white doctor coming towards her with the cruelly-poised needle. He loomed larger and larger until he seemed to blend into a great needle. She closed her eyes waiting to die. Nothing happened, she felt nothing. She opened her eyes slowly, hardly daring to hope that it was all over. She found to her agony, that the doctor was still there, poised needle and all. He was staring at her arm in distaste. Francie looked too. She saw a small white area on a dirty dark brown arm. She heard the doctor talking to the nurse.

"Filth, filth, filth, from morning to night. I know they're poor but they could wash. Water is free and soap is cheap. Just look at that arm, nurse."

The nurse looked and clucked in horror. Francie stood there with the hot flamepoints of shame burning her face. The doctor was a Harvard man, interning at the neighborhood hospital. Once a week, he was obligated to put in a few hours at one of the free clinics. He was going into a smart practice in Boston when his internship was over. Adopting the phraseology of the neighborhood, he referred to his Brooklyn internship as going through Purgatory when he wrote to his socially prominent fiancée in Boston.

The nurse was a Williamsburg girl. You could tell that by her accent. The child of poor Polish immigrants, she had been ambitious, worked days in a sweatshop and gone to school at night. Somehow she had gotten her training. She hoped some day to marry a doctor. She didn't want anyone to know she had come from the slums.

After the doctor's outburst, Francie stood hanging her head. She was a dirty girl. That's what the doctor meant. He was talking more quietly now asking the nurse how that kind of people could survive; that it would be a better world if they were all sterilized and couldn't breed anymore. Did that mean he wanted her to die? Would he do something to make her die because her hands and arms were dirty from the mud pies?

She looked at the nurse. To Francie, all women were mamas like her own mother and Aunt Sissy and Aunt Evy. She thought the nurse might say something like:

"Maybe this little girl's mother works and didn't have time to wash her good this morning," or, "You know how it is, Doctor, children *will* play in dirt." But what the nurse actually said was, "I know. Isn't it terrible? I sympathize with you, Doctor. There is no excuse for these people living in filth."

When the needle jabbed, Francie never felt it. The waves of hurt started by the doctor's words were racking her body and drove out all other feeling. While the nurse was expertly tying a strip of gauze around her arm and the doctor was putting his instrument in the sterilizer and taking out a fresh needle, Francie spoke up.

"My brother is next. His arm is just as dirty as mine so don't be surprised. And you don't have to tell him. You told me." They stared at this bit of humanity who had become so strangely articulate. Francie's voice went ragged with a sob. "You don't have to tell him. Besides it won't do no good. He's a boy and he don't care if he is dirty." She turned, stumbled a little and walked out of the room. As the door closed, she heard the doctor's surprised voice.

"I had no idea she'd understand what I was saying." She heard the nurse say, "Oh, well," on a sighing note.

From *Learning to Care.* Copyright © 1983 Scott, Foresman and Company.

# Problems

**1.** It is New Year's Day and your parents are taking you and your best friend to the Rose Parade. Your parents want you to sit with them, but you and your friend want to sit by yourselves. Your parents are worried that you might get lost in the crowd, but you feel that you are big enough to be on your own.

**2.** There are two characters in this situation, a teacher and a student named Jeff. Whenever anything goes wrong in class, no matter what it is, the teacher always blames Jeff. Sometimes the teacher is right. Jeff throws erasers, makes silly noises or teases the other kids. But lots of times the teacher is not right, and Jeff does not knock a neighbor's book off or kick the person sitting behind him. It's unfair to be scolded all the time, and the other kids don't get in trouble when they do the same things. Act out a situation in which the teacher and the student are interacting, representing the two different points of view. (Encourage the children involved in the enactment to play both the teacher and student roles.)

**3.** This situation involves two characters, a bully named Chuck and Chuck's friend Tony. Chuck clobbers everyone who doesn't do what he says. But Tony feels that kids shouldn't go around clobbering everyone in the neighborhood or at school, because that would make them bullies, and nobody likes a bully. How can Tony explain to Chuck that clobbering people doesn't solve anything very well? (You might want to briefly discuss the necessity to avoid "clobbering" anyone in these role-playing enactments. Again try to encourage the children to play both roles.)

**4.** An older sister and a younger sister are involved in this sitaution. The older sister has been running around with a crowd that her parents don't like. Last night, her parents went out and the older sister sneaked out with that group and went to a movie.

From *Learning to Care.* Copyright © 1983 Scott, Foresman and Company.